Billy the Kid

Billy the Kid

an anthology of tough verse

Michael Baldwin

Decorations by Dick Hart

CHAMPLAIN COLLEGE

HUTCHINSON

London Melbourne Sydney Auckland Johannesburg

Hutchinson & Co. (Publishers) Ltd

An imprint of the Hutchinson Publishing Group

17-21 Conway Street, London W1P 6JD

Hutchinson Group (Australia) Pty Ltd
30-32 Cremorne Street, Richmond South, Victoria 3121
PO Box 151, Broadway, New South Wales 2007

Hutchinson Group (NZ) Ltd
32-34 View Road, PO Box 40-086, Glenfield, Auckland 10

Hutchinson Group (SA) (Pty) Ltd
PO Box 337, Bergvlei 2012, South Africa

First published 1963
Eighth impression 1978
Reprinted 1980, 1982

Printed in Great Britain by litho
at The Anchor Press Ltd and bound by
Wm Brendon & Son Ltd
both of Tiptree, Essex

ISBN 0 09 067881 8

For
SUZANNE BRODIE

Acknowledgements

For permission to reprint copyright poems the editor is indebted to the following:

W. H. Auden and Faber & Faber Ltd for 'Victor was a little Baby' from COLLECTED SHORTER POEMS; John Bright for 'Death of a Whale' and 'Camp Fever'; W. Bridges-Adam for 'Notting Hill Polka'; Dr J. D. Bronowski for 'Man, Take your Gun' originally published in *New Writing*; John Lane the Bodley Head Ltd for 'Hialmar' from COLLECTED POEMS by Roy Campbell; Nancy Cato and Angus & Robertson Ltd for 'The Dead Swagman' from THE DANCING BOUGH; Charles Causley and Rupert Hart-Davis Ltd for 'Timothy Winters', 'Song of the Dying Gunner AAI' and 'Death of an Aircraft'; Richard Crust and the *Daily Mirror* for 'The Sad Story of Lefty and Ned' originally published in CHILDREN AS WRITERS; C. Day Lewis and Jonathan Cape Ltd for 'The Assertion' and 'Reconciliation' from WORD OVER ALL; Mrs H. M. Davies and Jonathan Cape Ltd for 'A Strange Meeting' and 'I am the poet, Davies, William' by W. H. Davies; the Literary Trustees of Walter de la Mare and the Society of Authors for 'Defeat' by Walter de la Mare; André Deutsch Ltd for 'Vergiss-meinicht' by Keith Douglas; Richard Eberhart and Chatto & Windus Ltd for 'The Fury of Aerial Bombardment' from SELECTED POEMS; Roy Fuller and André Deutsch Ltd for 'Socialist's Song' and 'Schwere Gustav'; Edward Arnold Ltd for 'Lord Gorbals', 'A Window-Cleaner in our Street' and 'Quiet Fun' by Harry Graham; Robert Graves, International Authors NV and Cassell & Co. Ltd for 'The

Oldest Soldier', 'Song: Lift-Boy' and 'Sergeant-Major Money' from COLLECTED POEMS 1953; W. Hart-Smith and Angus & Robertson Ltd for 'Black Stockman' from THE UNCEASING GROUND; the Society of Authors as the Literary Representative of the Estate of the late A. E. Housman and Jonathan Cape Ltd for 'A Shropshire Lad', 'The Carpenter's Son', 'The Culprit', 'Eight O'Clock' and 'Grenadier' from COLLECTED POEMS; Dorothy S. Howard for 'Birkett's Eagle'; Ted Hughes and Faber & Faber Ltd for 'Bayonet Charge' and 'Invitation to the Dance' from THE HAWK IN THE RAIN and 'The Bull Moses' from LUPERCAL; Seán Jennett and Faber & Faber Ltd for 'The Barge Horse' from THE CLOTH OF FLESH; Randall Jarrell and Faber & Faber Ltd for 'The Death of the Ball-Turret Gunner' from SELECTED POEMS; Mrs Bambridge and Methuen & Co. Ltd for 'Danny Deever' from BARRACK ROOM BALLADS by Rudyard Kipling; Irving Layton and the Ryerson Press for 'The Bull Calf'; John Lehmann (trans.) for 'Song of the Austrians in Dachau' by Georg Anders, originally published in *New Writing*; J. A. Lindon for 'A London Sparrow's If'; Mungo B. MacCallum for 'The Dream'; Louis MacNeice and Faber & Faber Ltd for 'Swing-Song' and 'The Streets of Laredo' from COLLECTED POEMS; Professor Charles Madge and Chatto & Windus Ltd for 'Blocking the Pass' from *Poems of Tomorrow*; Mrs Edgar Lee Masters and the Macmillan Co. of New York Inc. (1914, 1915, 1942) for 'Butch Weldy' from SPOON RIVER ANTHOLOGY by Edgar Lee Masters; W. S. Merwin and Oxford University Press for 'Burning the Cat'; James Michie and Rupert Hart-Davis Ltd for 'Arizona Nature Myth' from POSSIBLE LAUGHTER; Julian Mitchell and the *London Magazine* for 'Castaway'; Ogden Nash and J. M. Dent & Sons Ltd for 'Lather as you go' from FAMILY REUNION; Chatto & Windus Ltd for 'Dulce et Decorum Est' by Wilfred Owen; Coward-McCann Inc., N.Y., for 'The Ballad of Yukon Jake', copyright 1921, 1928 by Edward E. Paramore, renewed 1948 by

Edward E. Paramore, Jr.; Sylvia Plath, the *London Magazine* and William Heinemann Ltd for 'Snakecharmer'; William Plomer and Jonathan Cape Ltd for 'The Widow's Plot', 'The Murder on the Downs', 'The Dorking Thigh' and 'In the Snake Park'; John Pudney and Putnam & Co. Ltd for 'Ballad of the Long Drop', 'This Malefactor', 'Mediterranean War', 'Air Gunner' and 'Combat Report' from COLLECTED POEMS; Herbert Read and Faber & Faber Ltd for 'The Execution of Cornelius Vane' and 'Bombing Casualties in Spain' from COLLECTED POEMS; Peter Redgrove and Routledge & Kegan Paul Ltd for 'Gallows Bird'; The Ryerson Press for 'The Wrecker's Prayer' by Theodore Goodridge Roberts; Alan Ross and André Deutsch Ltd for 'Variety Girl' and 'Survivors'; Siegfried Sassoon for 'They', 'Counter-Attack', 'Wirers', 'Attack', 'Memorial Tablet' and 'The Hero'; Ernest Benn Ltd for 'The Shooting of Dan McGrew' by Robert Service; Angus & Robertson Ltd for 'Beach Burial' by Kenneth Slessor; Raymond Souster for 'Postcript', 'Drunk: On Crutches' and 'The Mother'; Stephen Spender and Faber & Faber Ltd for 'Thoughts during an Air-raid' from COLLECTED POEMS; Mrs Iris Wise and Macmillan & Co. Ltd for 'A Glass of Beer' from COLLECTED POEMS by James Stephens; Mrs Bertram Warr for 'The Heart to Carry On' by Bertram Warr; Judith Wright and Angus & Robertson Ltd for 'Drought Year' and 'Flood Year' from THE GATEWAY.

In addition, the editor and publishers have made every effort to trace the copyright holders of:

'Horny Hogan' by Robert Lowry; 'On the Swag' by R. A. K. Mason; 'The Spanish Hands' by L. J. Yates; and 'Two Poems (after A. E. Housman)' by Hugh Kingsmill.

Contents

COVES CROOKED AND STRAIGHT

Billy The Kid	Anon	21
Timothy Winters	Charles Causley	22
A Glass Of Beer	James Stephens	23
The Oldest Soldier	Robert Graves	24
Variety Girls	Alan Ross	25
Villon's Straight Tip	W. E. Henley	26
Faithless Nellie Gray	Thomas Hood	27
A Strange Meeting	W. H. Davies	30
The Yarn Of The 'Nancy Bell'	W. S. Gilbert	31
Poor But Honest	Anon	35
Lord Gorbals	Harry Graham	36
I Am The Poet, Davies, William	W. H. Davies	37
Socialist's Song	Roy Fuller	38
The Widow's Plot	William Plomer	39
Notting Hill Polka	W. Bridges-Adam	43
Horny Hogan	Robert Lowry	44
Drunk: On Crutches	Raymond Souster	46

STICKY ENDINGS

The Workhouse Boy	Anon	49
Dahn The Plug-'ole	Anon	50
The Sad Story Of Lefty And Ned	Richard Alan Crust	51
Framed In A First-Storey Winder . . .	Anon	53

A Window-Cleaner In Our Street	Harry Graham	54
A Close Thing	Anon	54
Frankie And Johnny	Anon	54
The Anarchist	Anon	58
Victor Was A Little Baby	W. H. Auden	58
Epitaph	Anon	64
Butch Weldy	Edgar Lee Masters	65
Song: Lift-Boy	Robert Graves	65
The Dying Airman	Anon	66
The Hearse Song	Anon	67
The Murder On The Downs	William Plomer	67
Lather As You Go	Ogden Nash	70
Quiet Fun	Harry Graham	71
The Dorking Thigh	William Plomer	71
Cheltenham Waters	Anon	73

TOUGH MEN, ROUGH PLACES

Greer County	Anon	77
Tying A Knot In The Devil's Tail	Anon	78
Defeat	Walter de la Mare	80
Blocking The Pass	Charles Madge	82
Paddy Murphy	Anon	83
Ballad Of Yukon Jake	Edward E. Paramore, Jr	83
Arizona Nature Myth	James Michie	89
Hialmar	Roy Campbell	90
Castaway	Julian Mitchell	92
The Wreckers' Prayer	Theodore Goodridge Roberts	92
The Shooting Of Dan McGrew	Robert Service	94
Drought Year	Judith Wright	98
Flood Year	Judith Wright	99
Birkett's Eagle	Dorothy S. Howard	99

The Dead Swagman　　　　　　　　Nancy Cato　102
Camp Fever　　　　　　　　　　　John Blight　103
Black Stockman　　　　　　　　W. Hart Smith　104
The Devil In Texas　　　　　　　　　　Anon　105
On The Swag　　　　　　　　R. A. K. Mason　106

THE EIGHT O'CLOCK WALK

Ballad Of The Long Drop　　　　　John Pudney　109
This Malefactor　　　　　　　　　John Pudney　110
The Faking Boy　　　　　　　　　　　Anon　111
The Culprit　　　　　　　　　A. E. Housman　111
Eight O'Clock　　　　　　　　A. E. Housman　112
The Epitaph In Form Of A Ballad　François Villon　113
Gallows Bird　　　　　　　　Peter Redgrove　114
Invitation To The Dance　　　　　Ted Hughes　115
A Shropshire Lad　　　　　　　A. E. Housman　116
The Carpenter's Son　　　　　　A. E. Housman　117
Two Poems (after A. E. Housman)　Hugh Kingsmill　119
Danny Deever　　　　　　　　Rudyard Kipling　120
Clever Tom Clinch　　　　　　　Jonathan Swift　121

SNAKES AND THINGS

In The Snake Park　　　　　　William Plomer　125
Snakecharmer　　　　　　　　　Sylvia Plath　126
Burning The Cat　　　　　　　W. S. Merwin　128
The Barge Horse　　　　　　　Seán Jennett　129
The Bull Moses　　　　　　　　Ted Hughes　130
Death Of A Whale　　　　　　　John Blight　131
The Bull Calf　　　　　　　　Irving Layton　132
Song　　　　　　　　　　　George Darley　133

A London Sparrow's If	J. A. Lindon	134
The Mother	Raymond Souster	135

WAR WAR WAR

I—The Soldiers

Vergissmeinicht	Keith Douglas	139
Reconciliation	C. Day Lewis	140
'They'	Siegfried Sassoon	141
The Dream	Mungo B. MacCallum	141
Postscript	Raymond Souster	142
Schwere Gustav	Roy Fuller	143
The Execution Of Cornelius Vane	Herbert Read	144
Sergeant-Major Money	Robert Graves	149
Bayonet Charge	Ted Hughes	150
Grenadier	A. E. Housman	151
Counter-Attack	Siegfried Sassoon	152
Wirers	Siegfried Sassoon	153
Attack	Siegfried Sassoon	154
Memorial Tablet	Siegfried Sassoon	155
Dulce et Decorum Est	Wilfred Owen	155

II—The Sailors

Song Of The Dying Gunner A.A.I.	Charles Causley	156
Survivors	Alan Ross	157
Beach Burial	Kenneth Slessor	158
Mediterranean War	John Pudney	159

III—The Airmen

The Heart To Carry On	Bertram Warr	160
Air Gunner	John Pudney	161

Combat Report   John Pudney   161
Handz Vos Mine Name   Anon   162
The Death Of The Ball-Turret Gunner   Randall Jarrell   162

IV—And The Civilians

The Spanish Hands   L. J. Yates   163
Song Of The Austrians In Dachau

           Georg Anders (tr. John Lehmann)   164
Death Of An Aircraft   Charles Causley   166
Swing-Song   Louis MacNeice   168
The Hero   Siegfried Sassoon   169
Bombing Casualties In Spain   Herbert Read   170
The Assertion   C. Day Lewis   171
The Streets Of Laredo   Louis MacNeice   172
The Fury Of Aerial Bombardment   Richard Eberhart   173
Thoughts During An Air Raid   Stephen Spender   174
Man, Take Your Gun   J. Bronowski   175

Introduction

THE flavour of this anthology can be quickly judged from a random selection of its titles: *The Wreckers' Prayer*, say, and *The Murder On The Downs*; or *Bombing Casualties In Spain* and *In The Snake Park*. These poems are, quite simply, works of strong excitement or bitter humour. This is a collection with a bias, and it has been made in the firm conviction that readers of secondary age (and older) prefer poems which are tough, vigorous and unsentimental, and which make a straightforward and immediate appeal.

Not all the authors are English, and many of them are not poets in the usual sense; nor is all they write poetry. Some of the verses are anonymous; some of them are ballads composed by American cowmen, by Australians from the Outback, by hoboes and layabouts and tramps; some of them have been written by ordinary men and women who have found their lives threatened by war; and at least one of them is the work of a child: but they have all been inspired (with the possible exception of Harry Graham) by the urgent conviction that they have something worth saying—something that matters enough to let the author forget the complicated idiom of the ego and concentrate wholeheartedly on his subject. Their words are often bald and their comments cryptic.

This is not to suppose that the poems included are sealed off in their own experience and that there is nothing educative, in the wider sense, in reading them. It would be impossible—to take a merely fanciful example—to compile a 'horror anthology' which would remain true to the criterion of poetry and at the same time be merely horror. And so it is here, however strong the meat. Thus John Pudney's magnificent poem *Ballad Of The Long Drop* may seem like an endless recital of violence, but the poet's genuine compassion and anger break through the Executioner's monologue, until in the end they take charge completely:

> *We dropped a girl who shot a bloke*
> *Because her heart was broke.*
>
> *Her heart was broke. She did him in*
> *For love: but love like hers is sin.*
> *We dropped her, for we drop them straight*
> *For love as well as hate.*

The whole problem of crime and punishment, of love and forgiveness, and of our collective and individual responsibility, faces us—not in the abstract, but as an experience in which we are involved.

And so it is with the war poetry, which includes in this case not only the poetry of soldiers, sailors, and airmen, but of civilians: the poetry of the victims of bombing raids, the inmates of concentration camps, and of the convicted labourers on a Spanish farm. A tapestry of horror? No: a fabric of men's thoughts in the face of horror, and again of men's urgent need at such moments to communicate, convince and exorcize. And in its turn, perhaps, the urgency of such themes most readily brings writer and reader together.

I should add that there are poems here—*Arizona Nature Myth* is an example—which do not clearly fit into the arrangement, but which nevertheless belong in spirit to the anthology as a whole, and have been unhesitatingly included. In the same way, although this anthology seeks—and I hope achieves—an original flavour, poems anthologized many times before, such as *Danny Deever*, which the teacher would automatically look for in the context of such a collection, have also been included.

MICHAEL BALDWIN

COVES CROOKED
AND STRAIGHT

Billy The Kid

Billy was a bad man
And carried a big gun,
He was always chasing women
And kept 'em on the run.

He shot men every morning
Just to make a morning meal—
If his gun ran out of bullets
He killed them with cold steel.

He kept folks in hot water,
And he stole from many a stage,
When his gut was full of liquor
He was always in a rage.

But one day he met a man
Who was a whole lot badder—
And now he's dead—
And we ain't none the sadder.

ANON. (AMERICAN BALLAD)

Timothy Winters

Timothy Winters comes to school
With eyes as wide as a football-pool,
Ears like bombs and teeth like splinters:
A blitz of a boy is Timothy Winters.

His belly is white, his neck is dark,
And his hair is an exclamation mark.
His clothes are enough to scare a crow
And through his britches the blue winds blow.

When teacher talks he won't hear a word
And he shoots down dead the arithmetic-bird,
He licks the patterns off his plate
And he's not even heard of the Welfare State.

Timothy Winters has bloody feet
And he lives in a house on Suez Street,
He sleeps in a sack on the kitchen floor
And they say there aren't boys like him any more.

Old man Winters likes his beer
And his missus ran off with a bombardier,
Grandma sits in the grate with a gin
And Timothy's dosed with an aspirin.

The Welfare Worker lies awake
But the law's as tricky as a ten-foot snake,
So Timothy Winters drinks his cup
And slowly goes on growing up.

At Morning Prayers the Headmaster helves
For children less fortunate than ourselves,
And the loudest response in the room is when
Timothy Winters roars 'Amen!'

So come one angel, come on ten:
Timothy Winters says 'Amen'
Amen amen amen amen.
Timothy Winters, Lord.

Amen.

CHARLES CAUSLEY

A Glass Of Beer

The lanky hank of a she in the inn over there,
Nearly killed me for asking the loan of a glass of beer;
May the devil grip the whey-faced slut by the hair,
And beat bad manners out of her skin for a year.

That parboiled ape, with the toughest jaw you will see
On virtue's path, and a voice that would rasp the dead,
Came roaring and raging the minute she looked at me,
And threw me out of the house on the back of my head!

If I asked her master he'd give me a cask a day;
But she, with the beer at hand, not a gill would arrange!
May she marry a ghost and bear him a kitten, and may
The High King of Glory permit her to get the mange.

JAMES STEPHENS
(from the Irish)

The Oldest Soldier

The sun shines warm on seven old soldiers
    Paraded in a row,
Perched like starlings on the railings—
    Give them plug-tobacco!

They'll croon you the Oldest-Soldier Song:
    Of Harry who took a holiday
From the sweat of ever thinking for himself
    Or going his own bloody way.

It was arms-drill, guard and kit-inspection,
    Like dreams of a long train-journey,
And the barrack-bed that Harry dossed on
    Went rockabye, rockabye, rockabye.

Harry kept his rifle and brasses clean,
    But Jesus Christ, what a liar!
He won the Military Medal
    For his coolness under fire.

He was never the last on parade
    Nor the first to volunteer,
And when Harry rose to be storeman
    He seldom had to pay for his beer.

Twenty-one years, and out Harry came
    To be odd-job man, or janitor,
Or commissionaire at a picture-house,
    Or, some say, bully to a whore.

But his King and Country calling Harry,
   He reported again at the Depot,
To perch on this railing like a starling,
   The oldest soldier of the row.

ROBERT GRAVES

Variety Girls

Sheila, Gloria, Billie, Noreen:
Going through the same routine,
Staring at the crumbling faience
Bright-eyed as we try to dance.

Saucy, playful, wicked minxes,
Expressionless in our art as Sphinxes;
We always get the bottom billing,
Flesh is weak but spirit willing.

One month called The Flirty Floozies,
Footlights on the latest bruises,
Next time known as Goodtime Girls,
Giggling under hennaed curls.

Each with slightly different charms,
Goodish legs *or* breasts *or* arms,
Beauties we have never been—
Sheila, Gloria, Billie, Noreen.

One thing no one ever could
Say is that we're any good,
Sandwiched in between scene changes
Kicking well within our ranges.

Yet we have our proper station,
A stable kind of reputation:
Opening shows but never nude,
Finale girls who'd think it rude

Undressing before the epicene:
Sheila, Gloria, Billie, Noreen.
Performing pets and comics alter,
We alone can never falter.

With mottled thighs and dusty knees
Getting through our 1–2–3's,
This week we're the Nightlife Nifties
Symbols of the Nineteen-Fifties.

But only the oldest patrons guess
What the programme doesn't confess,
That we were once The Nightclub Naughties
A decade before the Forties.

                                          ALAN ROSS

Villon's Straight Tip To All Cross Coves

Suppose you screeve? or go cheap-jack?
Or fake the broads? or fig a nag?
Or thimble-rig? or knap a yack?
Or pitch a snide? or smash a rag?
Suppose you duff? or nose and lag?
Or get the straight, and land your pot?
How do you melt the multy swag?
Booze and the blowens cop the lot.

Fiddle, or fence, or mace, or mack:
Or moskeneer, or flash the drag;
Dead-lurk a crib, or do a crack;
Pad with a slang, or chuck a fag;
Bonnet, or tout, or mump and gag;
Rattle the tats, or mark the spot;
You cannot bank a single stag;
Booze and the blowens cop the lot.

Suppose you try a different tack,
And on the square you flash your flag?
At penny-a-lining make your whack,
Or with the mummers mump and gag?
For nix, for nix the dibbs you bag!
At any graft, no matter what,
Your merry goblins soon stravag:
Booze and the blowens cop the lot.

It's up the spout and Charley Wag,
With wipes and tickers and what not,
Until the squeezer nips your scrag,
Booze and the blowens cop the lot.

W.E. HENLEY

Faithless Nellie Gray

Ben Battle was a soldier bold,
    And used to war's alarms;
But a cannon-ball took off his legs,
    So he laid down his arms.

Now as they bore him off the field,
   Said he, 'Let others shoot,
For here I leave my second leg,
   And the Forty-second Foot!'

The army-surgeons made him limbs:
   Said he:—'They're only pegs:
But there's as wooden members quite
   As represent my legs!'

Now Ben he loved a pretty maid,
   Her name was Nellie Gray:
So he went to pay her his devours
   When he'd devoured his pay!

But when he called on Nellie Gray,
   She made him quite a scoff;
And when she saw his wooden legs
   Began to take them off!

'O, Nellie Gray! O, Nellie Gray!
   Is this your love so warm?
The love that loves a scarlet coat
   Should be more uniform!'

She said, 'I loved a soldier once,
   For he was blythe and brave;
But I will never have a man
   With both legs in the grave!

'Before you had those timber toes,
   Your love I did allow,
But then, you know, you stand upon
   Another footing now!'

'O, Nellie Gray! O, Nellie Gray!
  For all your jeering speeches,
At duty's call, I left my legs
  In Badajos's *breaches*!'

'Why, then,' she said, 'you've lost
      the feet
  Of legs in war's alarms,
And now you cannot wear your shoes
  Upon your feats of arms!'

'Oh, false and fickle Nellie Gray;
  I know why you refuse:
Though I've no feet—some other man
  Is standing in my shoes!

'I wish I ne'er had seen your face;
  But now, a long farewell!
For you will be my death, alas!
  You will not be my *Nell*!'

Now when he went from Nellie Gray,
  His heart so heavy got---
And life was such a burthen grown,
  It made him take a knot!

So round his melancholy neck,
  A rope he did entwine,
And, for his second time in life,
  Enlisted in the Line!

One end he tied around a beam,
  And then removed his pegs,
And as his legs were off—of course,
  He soon was off his legs!

And there he hung, till he was dead
  As any nail in town,
For though distress had cut him up,
  It could not cut him down!

A dozen men sat on his corpse,
  To find out why he died—
And they buried Ben in four cross-
      roads,
  With a *stake* in his inside!

THOMAS HOOD

A Strange Meeting

The moon is full, and so am I;
  The night is late, the ale was good;
And I must go two miles and more
  Along a country road.

Now what is this that's drawing near?
  It seems a man, and tall;
But where the face should show its white
  I see no white at all.

Where is his face: or do I see
  The back part of his head,
And, with his face turned round about,
  He walks this way? I said.

He's close at hand, but where's the face?
    What devil is this I see?
I'm glad my body's warm with ale,
    There's trouble here for me.

I clutch my staff, I make a halt,
    'His blood or mine,' said I.
'Good night,' the black man said to me,
    As he went passing by.

W.H. DAVIES

The Yarn Of The 'Nancy Bell'

'Twas on the shores that round our coast
    From Deal to Ramsgate span,
That I found alone on a piece of stone
    An elderly naval man.

His hair was weedy, his beard was long,
    And weedy and long was he,
And I heard this wight on the shore recite,
    In a singular minor key:

'Oh, I am a cook and a captain bold,
    And the mate of the *Nancy* brig,
And a bo'sun tight, and a midshipmite,
    And the crew of the captain's gig.'

And he shook his fists and he tore his hair,
    Till I really felt afraid,
For I couldn't help thinking the man had been drinking,
    And so I simply said:

'Oh, elderly man, it's little I know
   Of the duties of men of the sea,
But I'll eat my hand if I understand
   How you can possibly be

'At once a cook, and a captain bold,
   And the mate of the *Nancy* brig,
And a bo'sun tight, and a midshipmite,
   And the crew of the captain's gig.'

Then he gave a hitch to his trousers, which
   Is a trick all seamen larn,
And having got rid of a thumping quid,
   He spun this painful yarn:

' 'Twas in the good ship *Nancy Bell*
   That we sailed to the Indian sea,
And there on a reef we come to grief
   Which has often occurred to me.

'And pretty nigh all o' the crew was drowned
   (There was seventy-seven o' soul),
And only ten of the *Nancy*'s men
   Said "Here!" to the muster-roll.

'There was me and the cook and the captain bold,
   And the mate of the *Nancy* brig,
And the bo'sun tight, and a midshipmite,
   And the crew of the captain's gig.

'For a month we'd neither wittles nor drink,
   Till a-hungry we did feel,
So we drawed a lot, and accordin' shot
   The captain for our meal.

'The next lot fell to the *Nancy*'s mate,
  And a delicate dish he made;
Then our appetite with the midshipmite
  We seven survivors stayed.

'And then we murdered the bo'sun tight,
  And he much resembled pig;
Then we wittled free, did the cook and me,
  On the crew of the captain's gig.

'Then only the cook and me was left,
  And the delicate question, "Which
Of us two goes to the kettle?" arose
  And we argued it out as sich.

'For I loved that cook as a brother, I did,
  And the cook he worshipped me;
But we'd both be blowed if we'd either be stowed
  In the other chap's hold, you see.

' "I'll be eat if you dines off me," says Tom,
  "Yes, that," says I, "you'll be,"—
"I'm boiled if I die, my friend," quoth I,
  And "Exactly so," quoth he.

'Says he, "Dear James, to murder me
  Were a foolish thing to do,
For don't you see that you can't cook *me*,
  While I can—and will—cook *you*!"

'So he boils the water, and takes the salt
  And the pepper in portions true
(Which he never forgot), and some chopped shalot,
  And some sage and parsley too.

' "Come here," says he, with a proper pride,
    Which his smiling features tell,
" 'Twill soothing be if I let you see
    How extremely nice you'll smell."

'And he stirred it round and round and round,
    And he sniffed at the foaming froth;
When I ups with his heels, and smothers his squeals
    In the scum of the boiling broth.

'And I eat that cook in a week or less,
    And—as I eating be
The last of his chops, why, I almost drops,
    For a wessel in sight I see!

        *   *   *   *   *   *

'And I never grin, and I never smile,
    And I never larf nor play,
But I sit and croak, and a single joke
    I have—which is to say:

'Oh, I am a cook and a captain bold,
    And the mate of the *Nancy* brig,
And a bosun tight, *and* a midshipmite,
    And the crew of the captain's gig!'

                                        W.S. GILBERT

Poor But Honest

She was poor, but she was honest,
  Victim of the squire's whim:
First he loved her, then he left her,
  And she lost her honest name.

Then she ran away to London,
  For to hide her grief and shame;
There she met another squire,
  And she lost her name again.

See her riding in her carriage,
  In the Park and all so gay:
All the nibs and nobby persons
  Come to pass the time of day.

See the little old-world village
  Where her aged parents live,
Drinking the champagne she sends them;
  But they never can forgive.

In the rich man's arms she flutters,
  Like a bird with broken wing:
First he loved her, then he left her,
  And she hasn't got a ring.

See him in the splendid mansion,
  Entertaining with the best,
While the girl that he has ruined,
  Entertains a sordid guest.

See him in the House of Commons,
   Making laws to put down crime,
While the victim of his passions
   Trails her way through mud and slime.

Standing on the bridge at midnight,
   She says: 'Farewell, blighted Love.'
There's a scream, a splash—Good Heavens!
   What is she a-doing of?

Then they drag her from the river,
   Water from her clothes they wrang,
For they thought that she was drownded;
   But the corpse got up and sang:

'It's the same the whole world over;
   It's the poor that gets the blame,
It's the rich that get the pleasure.
   Isn't it a blooming shame?'

                                              ANON.

Lord Gorbals

Once, as old Lord Gorbals motored
   Round his moors near John O' Groats,
He collided with a goatherd
   And a herd of forty goats.
By the time his car got through
They were all defunct but two.

Roughly he addressed the goatherd:
  'Dash my whiskers and my corns!
Can't you teach your goats, you dotard,
  That they ought to sound their horns?

Look, my A.A. badge is bent!
I've a mind to raise your rent!'

HARRY GRAHAM

I Am The Poet, Davies, William

I am the Poet, Davies, William,
  I sin without a blush or blink;
I am a man that lives to eat;
  I am a man that lives to drink.

My face is large, my lips are thick,
  My skin is coarse and black almost;
But the ugliest feature is my verse,
  Which proves my soul is black and lost.

Thank heaven thou didst not marry me,
  A poet full of blackest evil;
For how to manage my damned soul
  Will puzzle many a flaming devil.

W.H. DAVIES

Socialist's Song

It was an ex-sailor grown old in the war
Who'd learnt many swear words and how to tie knots,
A month in a barracks and then a month more,
A convoy between and some curious spots.
      Tattooed in Bombay
      Always short in his pay,
His wife never out of the family way.
Not early on duty but not really late;
Five fags and a parrot were all his estate.
Oh this is the man who must suffer the fate
Of being the only support of the state.

Demobbed with a mac and a smell of the truth,
A promise of peace and a couple of gongs,
And all that remained of six years of his youth,
Some dirty and some sentimental old songs.
      Then back to the shop,
      The two shilling hop,
And all the same faces still there at the top.
Still paid for the job at just under the rate,
A pint and a council house all his estate.
Oh this is the man who must suffer the fate
Of being the only support of the state.

Now what do you think, he is wanted again,
This teased-out old stripey with cracks in his neck;
He's wanted again for his muscle and brain—
The Oerlikon gun and an acre of deck.
      It may be the West
      That will lay him to rest
Or Asia provide him a watery vest;

Wherever he is on that terrible date
A fathom of canvas will be his estate.
For this is the man who must suffer the fate
Of being the only support of the state.

Can anything happen to add to the pleasure
Of life and improve the sad tone of this song?
Allow the ex-sailor to die at his leisure,
Decrease the superfluous measure of wrong?
    Yes, country and town
    Could turn upside down
Dislodging director, policeman and crown,
And fall in the lap of this man without hate—
Two hands and a family all his estate—
And truly permit him to suffer the fate
Of being the only support of the state.

ROY FULLER

The Widow's Plot

or, SHE GOT WHAT WAS COMING TO HER

Troubled was a house in Ealing
Where a widow's only son
Found her fond maternal feeling
    Overdone.

She was fussy and possessive;
Lennie, in his teens,
Found the atmosphere oppressive;
    There were scenes.

Tiring one day of her strictures,
Len went down the street,
Took a ticket at the pictures,
        Took his seat.

The picture was designed to thrill
But oh, the girl he sat beside!
If proximity could kill
        He'd have died.

Simple, sweet, sixteen and blonde,
Unattached, her name was Bess.
Well, boys, how would *you* respond?
        I can guess.

Len and Bessie found each other
All that either could desire,
But the fat, when he told Mother,
        Was in the fire.

The widow, who had always dreaded
This might happen, hatched a scheme
To smash, when they were duly wedded,
        Love's young dream.

One fine day she murmured, 'Sonny,
It's not for me to interfere,
You may think it rather funny
        But I hear

'Bess goes out with other men.'
'I don't believe it! It's a lie!
Tell me who with, where, and when?
      Tell my why?'

'Keep cool, Lennie, I suspected
That the girl was far from nice.
What a pity you rejected
      My advice.'

Suspicion from this fatal seed
Sprang up overnight
And strangled, like a poisonous weed,
      The lilies of delight.

Still unbelieving, Len believed
That Bess was being unchaste,
And a man that feels himself deceived
      May act in haste.

Now Bess was innocence incarnate
And never thought of other men;
She visited an aunt at Barnet
      Now and then,

But mostly stayed at home and dusted,
Crooning early, crooning late,
Unaware of being distrusted
      By her mate.

Then one day a wire was sent:
MEET ME PALACEUM AT EIGHT
URGENT AUNTIE. Bessie went
          To keep the date.

Slightly anxious, Bessie came
To the unusual rendezvous.
Desperate, Lennie did the same,
          He waited too,

Seeing but unseen by Bessie,
And in a minute seeing red—
For a stranger, fat and dressy,
          A trilby on his head,

In his tie a tasteful pearl,
On his face a nasty leer,
Sidled up towards the girl,
          And called her 'Dear,'

At this juncture Len stepped in,
Made a bee-line for the lout,
With a straight left to the chin
          Knocked him out.

He might have done the same for Bess
Thinking still that she had tricked him,
But she was gazing in distress
          At the victim.

'It's *her*!' she cried (but grammar
Never was her strongest suit):
'She's passed out!' he heard her stammer,
        'Lennie, scoot!'

'It's *what*? A *her*? Good God, it's *Mum*!
Ah, now I see! A wicked plan
To make me think my Bess had come
        To meet a *man*—'

'Now what's all this?' a copper said,
Shoving the crowd aside. 'I heard a
Rumour somebody was dead.
        Is it murder?'

Len quite candidly replied,
'No, officer, it's something less.
It's justifiable matricide,
        Isn't it, Bess?'

                                        WILLIAM PLOMER

Notting Hill Polka

We've—had—
A Body in the house
    Since father passed away:
He took bad on
Saturday night an' he
    Went the followin' day.

Mum's—pulled—
The blinds all down
   An' bought some Sherry Wine,
An' we've put the tin
What the Arsenic's in
   At the bottom of the Ser-pen-tine!

W. BRIDGES-ADAM

Horny Hogan

A FEELTHY POME

Critchers! Horny Hogan sayed
& walked his beat—beat his walk
& saw loif larf, loif cree—
Critchers! Horny scorfed, and spart.

Oi arm the cocker here! Moi
brarss poilished & moi gon in order
Oi arm the cocker, mocker, bocker,
jocker of em all.

Bibies, little winch, twinty-foive
pinnies fer a chonk of luv—
lovers, sodgers, shoppers, sharpers,
mogs pinny-woise & por

lil ones so hoi what nid pertixion—
Oi arm the cocker here! Horny
Hogan sayed.Oi'll sive the larsies,
Oi'll kip the fithe!

Didee? Did Horny Hogan kip it?
Did Horny Hogan kip the larsies
sife and sound from ivil? Woulduv,
rilly woulduv but that he loiked to flarndle

Loiked to flup too much, did Horny,
fer a cop, pertected blonduns,
riduns & brunettes, gave em
the long orm of the lar

Overdid it somut, did Cocker
Mocker Horny Hogan—gave full pertixion to
one too miny ridid, one too miny
blornde—did it ifter hours ivin

till the Force foundim daid one
cool sprin mornin, still pertictin, still
kipin the fithe, shot at his post in a

tinth strit room, the horsband disappeared
& the blornde there wippin—
Horny Hogan daid! Horny
Hogan—kipper of the fithe

Horny Hogan, the cocker mocker of em all.

ROBERT LOWRY

Drunk: On Crutches

Simply being drunk makes it
Tough enough to get around,
But a guy hobbling on crutches—
How does he figure it at all?
The point is
He doesn't; and like this one now
Will be doing good if he goes
Six lamp-posts; or make it
Ten if you like a sure thing.
Which reminds me of horses and also
The plain fact that a horse
Does better in the world
Than most humans in it.
Like this one now: this corpse,
This living death coming toward you.

RAYMOND SOUSTER

STICKY ENDINGS

The Workhouse Boy

The cloth was laid in the Vorkhouse hall,
The great-coats hung on the white-wash'd wall;
The paupers all were blithe and gay,
Keeping their Christmas holiday,
When the Master he cried with a roguish leer,
'You'll all get fat on your Christmas cheer!'
When one by his looks did seem to say,
'I'll have some more soup on this Christmas-day.'
        Oh the Poor Vorkhouse Boy.

At length, all on us to bed vos sent,
The boy vos missing—in search ve vent:
Ve sought him above, ve sought him below,
Ve sought him with faces of grief and woe;
Ve sought him that hour, ve sought him that night;
Ve sought him in fear, and ve sought him in fright,
Ven a young pauper cried 'I knows ve shall
Get jolly vell vopt for losing our pal.'
        Oh the Poor Vorkhouse Boy.

Ve sought in each corner, each crevice ve knew;
Ve sought down the yard, ve sought up the flue;
Ve sought in each kettle, each saucepan, each pot,
In the water-butt look'd, but found him not.
And veeks roll'd on;—ve vere all of us told
That somebody said, he'd been burk'd and sold;

49

Ven our Master goes out, the Parishiners vild
Cry 'There goes the cove that burk'd the poor child.'
            Oh the Poor Vorkhouse Boy.

At length the soup copper repairs did need,
The Coppersmith came, and there he seed,
A dollop of bones lay a-grizzling there,
In the leg of the breeches the poor boy did vear!
To gain his fill the boy did stoop,
And dreadful to tell, he was boil'd in the soup!
And ve all of us say, and ve say it sincere,
That he was push'd in there by an overseer.
            Oh the Poor Vorkhouse Boy.

                                            ANON.

Dahn The Plug-'ole

A muvver was barfin' 'er biby one night,
The youngest of ten and a tiny young mite,
The muvver was pore and the biby was thin,
Only a skelington covered in skin;
The muvver turned rahnd for the soap orf the rack,
She was but a moment, but when she turned back,
The biby was gorn; and in anguish she cried,
'Oh, where is my biby?'—the Angels replied:
'Your biby 'as fell dahn the plug-'ole,
Your biby 'as gorn dahn the plug;
The poor little thing was so skinny and thin
'E oughter been barfed in a jug;

Your biby is perfectly 'appy,
'E won't need a barf any more,
Your biby 'as fell dahn the plug-'ole,
Not lorst, but gorn before!'

ANON.

The Sad Story Of Lefty And Ned

There were two crooks, called Lefty and Ned,
Who had to steal for their daily bread.
But now their bodies are under the ground,
Left there to rot until they're found.

One day they planned to rob the bank,
The other side of the taxi-rank.
But now their bodies are under the ground
Left there to rot until they're found.

And then they tunnelled into the bank,
The other side of the taxi-rank.
But now their bodies are under the ground,
Left there to rot until they're found.

I think it was Monday they got through,
With all their tools and gelignite too.
But now their bodies are under the ground,
Left there to rot until they're found.

They put the gelignite in its place,
With a mattress on top, just in case.
But now their bodies are under the ground,
Left there to rot until they're found.

And then they had a terrible scare,
When the Burglar alarm rent the air.
But now their bodies are under the ground,
Left there to rot until they're found.

Back to the tunnel they made their way,
Just as the police joined in the fray.
But now their bodies are under the ground,
Left there to rot until they're found.

Ned dropped the torch as he shut the hatch,
Because of the dark, he struck a match.
But now their bodies are under the ground,
Left there to rot until they're found.

But he'd forgotten the gelignite,
And right on to it he dropped the light.
So now their bodies are under the ground,
Left there to rot until they're found.

So now they're dead, the tunnel's caved in,
This is the punishment for their sin.
And now their bodies are under the ground,
Left there to rot until they're found.

And now the moral, Crime Never Pays,
You'd best take note of this worthy phrase.
Because their bodies are under the ground,
Left there to rot until they're found.

RICHARD ALAN CRUST
(Age 12)

Framed In A First-Storey Winder . . .

Framed in a first-storey winder of a burnin' buildin'
Appeared: A Yuman Ead!
Jump into this net, wot we are 'oldin'
And yule be quite orl right!

But 'ee wouldn't jump . . .

And the flames grew Igher and Igher and Igher.
(Phew!)

Framed in a second-storey winder of a burnin' buildin'
Appeared: A Yuman Ead!
Jump into this net, wot we are 'oldin'
And yule be quite orl right!

But 'ee wouldn't jump . . .

And the flames grew Igher and Igher and Igher
(Strewth!)

Framed in a third-storey winder of a burnin' buildin'
Appeared: A Yuman Ead!
Jump into this net, wot we are 'oldin'
And yule be quite orl right!
Honest!

And 'ee jumped . . .

And 'ee broke 'is bloomin' neck!

ANON.

A Window-Cleaner In Our Street

A window-cleaner in our street
Who fell (five storeys) at my feet
Impaled himself on my umbrella.
I said: 'Come, come, you careless fella!
If my umbrella had been shut
You might have landed on my nut.'

                                          HARRY GRAHAM

A Close Thing

Smith Minor, whose first name was Paul,
Just narrowly missed a bad fall—
He broke several teeth
And the jawbone beneath,
Seven ribs, and a leg, but that's all!

                                          ANON.

Frankie And Johnny

Frankie and Johnny were lovers.
O my Gawd how they did love!
They swore to be true to each other,
As true as the stars above.
He was her man but he done her wrong.

Frankie went down to the hock-shop,
Went for a bucket of beer,
Said: 'O Mr Bartender
Has my loving Johnny been here?
He is my man but he's doing me wrong.'

'I don't want to make you no trouble,
I don't want to tell you no lie,
But I saw Johnny an hour ago
With a girl named Nelly Bly,
He is your man but he's doing you wrong.'

Frankie went down to the hotel,
She didn't go there for fun,
'Cause underneath her kimona
She toted a 44 Gun.
He was her man but he done her wrong.

Frankie went down to the hotel.
She rang the front-door bell,
Said: 'Stand back all you chippies
Or I'll blow you all to hell.
I want my man for he's doing me wrong.'

Frankie looked in through the key-hole
And there before her eye
She saw her Johnny on the sofa
A-loving up Nelly Bly.
He was her man; he was doing her wrong.

Frankie threw back her kimona,
Took out a big 44,
Root-a-toot-toot, three times she shoot
Right through that hardware door.
He was her man but he was doing her wrong.

Johnny grabbed up his Stetson,
Said: 'O my Gawd Frankie don't shoot!'
But Frankie pulled hard on the trigger
And the gun went root-a-toot-toot.
She shot her man who was doing her wrong.

'Roll me over easy,
Roll me over slow,
Roll me over on my right side
Cause my left side hurts me so.
I was her man but I done her wrong.'

'Bring out your rubber-tired buggy,
Bring out your rubber-tired hack;
I'll take my Johnny to the graveyard
But I won't bring him back.
He was my man but he done me wrong.

'Lock me in that dungeon,
Lock me in that cell,
Lock me where the north-east wind
Blows from the corner of Hell.
I shot my man 'cause he done me wrong.'

It was not murder in the first degree,
It was not murder in the third.
A woman simply shot her man
As a hunter drops a bird.
She shot her man 'cause he done her wrong.

Frankie said to the Sheriff,
'What do you think they'll do?'
The Sheriff said to Frankie,
'It's the electric-chair for you.
You shot your man 'cause he done you wrong.'

Frankie sat in the jail-house,
Had no electric fan,
Told her sweet little sister:
'There ain't no good in a man.
I had a man but he done me wrong.'

Once more I saw Frankie,
She was sitting in the Chair
Waiting for to go and meet her God
With the sweat dripping out of her hair.
He was a man but he done her wrong.

This story has no moral,
This story has no end,
This story only goes to show
That there ain't no good in men.
He was her man but he done her wrong.

ANON.

The Anarchist

A Bolshie, the World's Very Worst,
For everyone's gore was athirst:
He placed a big bomb
With Satanic aplomb
And went off—but the bomb went off first!

ANON.

Victor Was A Little Baby

(Tune: 'FRANKIE AND JOHNNY')

Victor was a little baby,
    Into this world he came;
His father took him on his knee and said,
    'Don't dishonour the family name.'

Victor looked up at his father
    Looked up with big round eyes:
His father said, 'Victor, my only son,
    Don't you ever ever tell lies.'

Victor and his father went riding
    Out in a little dog-cart;
His father took a Bible from his pocket and read,
    'Blessed are the pure in heart.'

It was a frosty December,
　　It wasn't the season for fruits;
His father fell dead of heart disease
　　While lacing up his boots.

It was a frosty December
　　When into his grave he sank;
His uncle found Victor a post as cashier
　　In the Midland Counties Bank.

It was a frosty December
　　Victor was only eighteen,
But his figures were neat and his margins straight
　　And his cuffs were always clean.

He took a room at the Peveril,
　　A respectable boarding-house;
And Time watched Victor day after day
　　As a cat will watch a mouse.

The clerks slapped Victor on the shoulder;
　　'Have you ever had a woman?' they said,
'Come down town with us on Saturday night.'
　　Victor smiled and shook his head.

The manager sat in his office,
　　Smoked a Corona cigar;
Said, 'Victor's a decent fellow but
　　He's too mousey to go far.'

Victor went up to his bedroom,
   Set the alarum bell;
Climbed into bed, took his Bible and read
   Of what happened to Jezebel.

It was the First of April,
   Anna to the Peveril came;
Her eyes, her lips, her breasts, her hips
   And her smile set men aflame.

She looked as pure as a schoolgirl
   On her First Communion day
But her kisses were like the best champagne
   When she gave herself away.

It was the Second of April,
   She was wearing a coat of fur;
Victor met her upon the stairs
   And he fell in love with her.

The first time he made his proposal,
   She laughed, said, 'I'll never wed';
The second time there was a pause;
   Then she smiled and shook her head.

Anna looked into her mirror,
   Pouted and gave a frown:
Said, 'Victor's as dull as a wet afternoon
   But I've got to settle down.'

The third time he made his proposal,
  As they walked by the Reservoir:
She gave him a kiss like a blow on the head,
  Said, 'You are my heart's desire.'

They were married early in August,
  She said, 'Kiss me, you funny boy':
Victor took her in his arms and said,
  'O my Helen of Troy.'

It was the middle of September,
  Victor came to the office one day;
He was wearing a flower in his buttonhole,
  He was late but he was gay.

The clerks were talking of Anna,
  The door was just ajar:
One said, 'Poor old Victor, but where ignorance
  Is bliss, et cetera.'

Victor stood still as a statue,
  The door was just ajar:
One said, 'God, what fun I had with her
  In that Baby Austin car.'

Victor walked out into the High Street,
  He walked to the edge of the town;
He came to the allotments and the rubbish heaps
  And his tears came tumbling down.

Victor looked up at the sunset
  As he stood there all alone;
Cried, 'Are you in Heaven, Father?'
  But the sky said, 'Address not known'.

Victor looked up at the mountains,
  The mountains all covered with snow:
Cried, 'Are you pleased with me, Father?'
  And the answer came back, 'No'.

Victor came to the forest,
  Cried, 'Father, will she ever be true?'
And the oaks and the beeches shook their heads
  And they answered, 'Not to you'.

Victor came to the meadow
  Where the wind went sweeping by:
Cried, 'O Father, I love her so,'
  But the wind said, 'She must die.'

Victor came to the river
  Running so deep and so still:
Crying, 'O Father, what shall I do?'
  And the river answered, 'Kill'.

Anna was sitting at a table,
  Drawing cards from a pack;
Anna was sitting at table
  Waiting for her husband to come back.

It wasn't the Jack of Diamonds
   Nor the Joker she drew at first;
It wasn't the King or the Queen of Hearts
   But the Ace of Spades reversed.

Victor stood in the doorway,
   He didn't utter a word:
She said, 'What's the matter, darling?'
   He behaved as if he hadn't heard.

There was a voice in his left ear,
   There was a voice in his right,
There was a voice at the base of his skull
   Saying, 'She must die tonight'.

Victor picked up a carving-knife,
   His features were set and drawn,
Said, 'Anna, it would have been better for you
   If you had not been born.'

Anna jumped up from the table,
   Anna started to scream,
But Victor came slowly after her
   Like a horror in a dream.

She dodged behind the sofa,
   She tore down a curtain rod,
But Victor came slowly after her:
   Said, 'Prepare to meet thy God.'

She managed to wrench the door open,
    She ran and she didn't stop.
But Victor followed her up the stairs
    And he caught her at the top.

He stood there above the body,
    He stood there holding the knife;
And the blood ran down the stairs and sang,
    'I'm the Resurrection and the Life'.

They tapped Victor on the shoulder,
    They took him away in a van;
He sat as quiet as a lump of moss
    Saying, 'I am the Son of Man'.

Victor sat in a corner
    Making a woman of clay:
Saying, 'I am Alpha and Omega, I shall come
    To judge the earth one day.'

                                                    W.H. AUDEN

Epitaph

Here lies a man who was killed by lightning.
He died when his prospects seemed to be brightening.
He might have cut a flash in this world of trouble,
But the flash cut him, and he lies in the stubble.

                                                    ANON.

Butch Weldy

After I got religion and steadied down
They gave me a job in the canning works,
And every morning I had to fill
The tank in the yard with gasoline,
That fed the blow-fires in the sheds
To heat the soldering irons.
And I mounted a rickety ladder to do it,
Carrying buckets full of the stuff.
One morning, as I stood there pouring,
The air grew still and seemed to heave,
And I shot up as the tank exploded,
And down I came with both legs broken,
And my eyes burned crisp as a couple of eggs.
For someone left a blow-fire going,
And something sucked the flame in the tank.
The Circuit Judge said whoever did it
Was a fellow-servant of mine, and so
Old Rhodes' son didn't have to pay me.
And I sat on the witness stand as blind
As Jack the Fiddler, saying over and over,
'I didn't know him at all.'

EDGAR LEE MASTERS

Song : Lift-Boy

Let me tell you the story of how I began:
I began as the knife-boy and ended as the boot-man,
With nothing in my pockets but a jack-knife and a button,
With nothing in my pockets but a jack-knife and a button,
With nothing in my pockets.

Let me tell you the story of how I went on:
I began as the lift-boy and ended as the lift-man,
With nothing in my pockets but a jack-knife and a button,
With nothing in my pockets but a jack-knife and a button,
With nothing in my pockets.

I found it very easy to whistle and play
With nothing in my head or my pockets all day,
With nothing in my pockets.

But along came Old Eagle, like Moses or David,
He stopped at the fourth floor and preached me Damnation:
'Not a soul shall be savèd, not one shall be savèd.
The whole First Creation shall forfeit salvation:
From knife-boy to lift-boy, from raggèd to regal,
Not one shall be saved, not you, not Old Eagle,
No soul on earth escapeth, even if all repent—'
So I cut the cords of the lift and down we went,
With nothing in our pockets.

ROBERT GRAVES

The Dying Airman

A handsome young airman lay dying,
And as on the aerodrome he lay,
To the mechanics who round him came sighing,
These last dying words he did say:

'Take the cylinders out of my kidneys,
Take the connecting-rod out of my brains,
Take the cam-shaft from out of my backbone,
And assemble the engine again.'

ANON.

The Hearse Song

The old Grey Hearse goes rolling by,
You don't know whether to laugh or cry;
For you know some day it'll get you too,
And the hearse's next load may consist of you.

They'll take you out, and they'll lower you down,
While men with shovels stand all around;
They'll throw in dirt, and they'll throw in rocks,
And they won't give a damn if they break the box.

And your eyes drop out and your teeth fall in,
And the worms crawl over your mouth and chin;
They invite their friends and their friends' friends too
And you look like hell when they're through with you.

ANON.

The Murder On The Downs

Past a cow and past a cottage,
Past the sties and byres,
Past the equidistant poles
Holding taut the humming wires,

Past the inn and past the garage,
Past the hypodermic steeple
Ever ready to inject
The opium of the people,

In the fresh, the Sussex morning,
Up the Dangerous Corner lane
Bert and Jennifer were walking
Once again.

The spider's usual crochet
Was caught upon the thorns,
The skylark did its stuff,
The cow had horns.

'See,' said Bert, 'my hand is sweating.'
With her lips she touched his palm
As they took the path above the
Valley farm.

Over the downs the wind unveiled
That ancient monument the sun,
And a perfect morning
Had begun.

But summer lightning like an omen
Carried on a silent dance
On his heart's horizon, as he
Gave a glance

At the face beside him, and she turned
Dissolving in his frank blue eyes
All her hope, like aspirin.
On that breeding-place of lies

His forehead, too, she laid her lips.
'Let's find a place to sit,' he said.
'Past the gorse, down in the bracken
Like a bed.'

Oh the fresh, the laughing morning!
Warmth upon the bramble brake
Like a magnet draws from darkness
A reviving snake:

Just an adder, slowly gliding,
Sleepy curving idleness,
On the Sussex turf now writing
S O S.

Jennifer in sitting, touches
With her hand an agaric,
Like a bulb of rotten rubber
Soft and thick,

Screams, withdraws, and sees its colour
Like a leper's liver,
Leans on Bert so he can feel her
Shiver.

Over there the morning ocean,
Frayed around the edges, sighs,
At the same time gaily twinkles,
Conniving with a million eyes

At Bert whose free hand slowly pulls
A rayon stocking from his coat,
Twists it quickly, twists it neatly
Round her throat.

'Ah, I knew that this would happen!'
Her last words: and not displeased
Jennifer relaxed, still smiling
While he squeezed.

Under a sky without a cloud
Lay the still unruffled sea,
And in the bracken like a bed
The murderee.

WILLIAM PLOMER

Lather As You Go

Beneath this slab
John Brown is stowed.
He watched the ads
And not the road.

OGDEN NASH

Quiet Fun

My son Augustus, in the street, one day,
  Was feeling quite exceptionally merry.
A stranger asked him: 'Can you tell me, pray,
  The quickest way to Brompton Cemetery?'
'The quickest way? You bet I can!' said Gus,
  And pushed the fellow underneath a bus.

*   *   *   *   *

Whatever people say about my son,
He does enjoy his little bit of fun.

HARRY GRAHAM

The Dorking Thigh

About to marry and invest
Their lives in safety and routine
Stanley and June required a nest
And came down on the 4.15.

The agent drove them to the Posh Estate
And showed them several habitations.
None did. The afternoon got late
With questions, doubts, and explanations.

Then day grew dim and Stan fatigued
And disappointment raised its head,
But June declared herself intrigued
To know where that last turning led.

It led to a Tudor snuggery styled
'Ye Kumfi Nooklet' on the gate.
'A gem of a home,' the salesman smiled,
'My pet place on the whole estate;

'It's not quite finished, but you'll see
Good taste itself.' They went inside.
'This little place is built to be
A husband's joy, a housewife's pride.'

They saw the white convenient sink,
The modernistic chimney-piece,
June gasped for joy, Stan gave a wink
To say, 'Well, here our quest can cease.'

The salesman purred (he'd managed well)
And June undid a cupboard door.
'For linen,' she beamed. And out there fell
A nameless Something on the floor.

'Something the workmen left, I expect,'
The agent said, as it fell at his feet,
Nor knew that his chance of a sale was wrecked.
'Good heavens, it must be a joint of meat!'

Ah yes, it was meat, it was meat all right,
A joint those three will never forget—
For they stood alone in the Surrey night
With the severed thigh of a plump brunette . . .

*　　　*　　　*　　　*　　　*

Early and late, early and late,
Traffic was jammed round the Posh Estate,
And the papers were full of the Dorking Thigh
And who, and when, and where, and why.

A trouser button was found in the mud
(Who made it? Who wore it? Who lost it? Who knows?)
But no one found a trace of blood
Or her body or face, or the spoiler of those.

He's acting a play in the common air
On which no curtain can ever come down.
Though 'Ye Kumfi Nooklet' was shifted elsewhere
June made Stan take a flat in town.

WILLIAM PLOMER

Cheltenham Waters

Here lie I and my four daughters
Killed by drinking Cheltenham waters.
Had we but stuck to Epsom salts,
    We wouldn't have been in these here vaults.

ANON.

TOUGH MEN, ROUGH PLACES

Greer County

How happy am I when I crawl into bed—
A rattlesnake hisses a tune at my head,
A gay little centipede, all without fear,
Crawls over my pillow and into my ear.

My clothes is all raggéd as my language is rough,
My bread is corn-dodgers, both solid and tough;
But yet I am happy, and live at my ease
On sorghum molasses, bacon, and cheese.

Good-bye to Greer County where blizzards arise,
Where the sun never sinks and a flea never dies,
And the wind never ceases but always remains
Till it starves us to death on our government claims.

Farewell to Greer County, farewell to the West,
I'll travel back East to the girl I love best,
I'll travel back to Texas and marry me a wife,
And quit cornbread for the rest of my life.

ANON.

Tying A Knot In The Devil's Tail

Way up high in the Syree Peaks
Where the yellow pines grow tall,
Old Sandy Bob and Buster Jiggs
Had a round-up camp last fall.

They took their horses and their runnin' irons
And maybe a dog or two;
And they 'lowed they'd brand all the long-eared calves
That came within their view.

Many a long-eared dogie
That didn't hush up by day
Had his long ears whittled and his old hide scorched
In a most artistic way.

One fine day, says Buster Jiggs
As he throwed his cigo down,
'I'm tired o' cow-piography
And I 'lows I'm goin' to town.'

So they saddles up and they hits a lope
Fer it wa'n't no sight of a ride,
And them was the days that a good cow-punch'
Could ile up his inside.

They started her in at the Kentucky Bar
At the head of Whisky Row
And ends her up at the Depot House,
Some forty drinks below.

They sets her up and they turns around
And goes her the other way;
An' to tell the God-forsaken truth
Them boys got tight that day.

When they were on their way to camp
A-packin' a pretty good load,
Who should they meet but the Devil hisself
Come a-prancin' down the road.

Says he, 'Ye ornery cowbow skunks,
Ye'd better hunt for your holes,
'Cause I've come up from hell's rim-rock
To gather in your souls.'

Says Buster Jiggs: 'The Devil be damned!
We boys are feelin' kinda tight,
But you don't gather any cowboy souls
Unless you want a fight.'

So he punches a hole in his old cigo
And he throws her straight and true
An' he loops it over the Devil's horns
An' he takes his dallies true.

Old Sandy Bob was a riata-man
With his gut-line coiled up neat,
But he shakes her out, an' builds a loop
An' he ropes the Devil's hind feet.

They stretches him out and they tails him down,
An' while their irons were gettin' hot
They cropped and swallow-forked his ears
An' branded him up a lot.

They prunes him up with a dehorning saw
An' they knotted his tail for a joke;
An' then they rode off an' left him there
Tied up to a lilac-jack oak.

Now when you're way up high in the Syree Peaks
An' you hear one hell of a wail,
It's only the Devil a-bellerin' round
About those knots in his tail.

ANON.

Defeat

The way on high burned white beneath the sun,
Crag and gaunt pine stood stark in windless heat,
With sun-parched weeds its stones were over-run,
And he who had dared it, his long journey done,
Lay sunken in the slumber of defeat.

A raven low in the air, with stagnant eyes,
Poised in the instant of alighting gust,
Rent the thin silence with his hungry cries,
Voicing his greed o'er this far-scented prize,
Stiff in the invisible movement of the dust.

He lay, sharp-boned beneath his skin, half-nude,
His black hair tangled with a blackening red,
His gaze wide-staring in his solitude,
O'er which a bristling cloud of flies did brood,
In mumbling business with his heedless head.

Unfathomable drifts of space below,
Stretched, like a grey glass, an infinite low sea,
Whereon a conflict of bright beams did flow,
In fiery splendour trembling to and fro—
The noon sun's angel-loosened archery.

And still on high, the way, a lean line, wound,
Wherefrom the raven had swooped down to eat,
To mortal eyes without an end, or bound,
Nor any creeping shadow to be found
To cool the sunken temples of defeat.

Defeat was scrawled upon each naked bone,
Defeat in the glazed vacancy of his eye,
Defeat his hand clutched in that waste of stone,
Defeat the bird yelped, and the flies' mazed drone
Lifted thanksgivingly for defeat come by.

Lost in eternal rumination stare
Those darkened sockets of a dreamless head,
That cheek and jaw with the unpeopled air,
With smile immutable, unwearying, share
The subtle cogitations of the dead.

Yet, dwindling mark upon fate's viewless height,
For sign and token above the infinite sea,
'Neath the cold challenge of the all-circling night
Shall lie for witness in the Invisible's sight
The mockless victory that defeat may be.

WALTER DE LA MARE

Blocking The Pass

With an effort Grant swung the great block,
The swivel operated and five or six men
Crouched under the lee of the straight rock.

They waited in silence or counting ten,
They thrust their fingers in their wet hair,
The steel sweated in their hands. And then

The clouds hurried across a sky quite bare,
The sounds of the station, three miles off, ceased,
The dusty birds hopped keeping watch. And there

Arose to what seemed as high as the sky at least,
Arose a giant and began to die,
Arose such a shape as the night in the East.

The stones sobbed, the trees gave a cry,
A tremulous wonder shook animal and plant,
And a decapitating anger stirred the sky

And alone, on a tall stone, stood Grant.

CHARLES MADGE

Paddy Murphy

The night that Paddy Murphy died
I never shall forget!
The whole damn town got stinking drunk
And they're not sober yet.

There is one thing they did that night
That filled me full of fear:
They took the ice right off the corpse
And stuck it in the beer.

That's how they showed their respect for
    Paddy Murphy,
That's how they showed their honour and their
    fight,
That's how they showed their respect for
    Paddy Murphy
They drank his health in ice-cold beer that
    night!

ANON.

Ballad Of Yukon Jake

(THE HERMIT OF SHARK TOOTH SHOAL)

Oh the North Countree is a hard countree
    That mothers a bloody brood;
And its icy arms hold hidden charms
    For the greedy, the sinful and lewd.

And strong men rust, from the gold and lust
    That sears the Northland soul,
But the wickedest born, from the Pole to the Horn,
    Is the Hermit of Shark Tooth Shoal.

Now Jacob Kaime was the Hermit's name,
    In the days of his pious youth,
Ere he cast a smirch on the Baptist Church
    By betraying a girl named Ruth.

But now men quake at Yukon Jake,
    The Hermit of Sharp Tooth Shoal,
For that is the name that Jacob Kaime
    Is known by from Nome to the Pole.

He was just a boy and the parson's joy
    (Ere he fell for the gold and the muck),
And he learned to pray, with the hogs and hay
    On a farm near Keokuk.

But a Service tale of illicit kale—
    And whisky and women wild—
Drained the morals clean as a soup-tureen
    From this poor but honest child.

He longed for the bite of a Yukon night
    And the Northern Light's weird flicker,
For a game of stud in the frozen mud,
    And the taste of raw red licker.

He wanted to mush along in the slush
   With a team of husky hounds,
And to fire his gat at a beaver hat
   And knock it out of bounds.

So he left his home for the hell-town Nome
   On Alaska's ice-ribbed shores,
And he learned to curse and to drink and worse—
   Till the rum dripped from his pores.

When the boys on a spree were drinking it free
   In a Malamute saloon
And Dan McGrew and his dangerous crew
   Shot craps with the piebald coon:

When the Kid on his stool banged away like a fool
   At a jag-time melody
And the bar-keep vowed to the hardboiled crowd
   That he'd cree-mate Sam McGee—

Then Jacob Kaime, who had taken the name
   Of Yukon Jake, the Killer,
Would rake the dive with his forty-five
   Till the atmosphere grew chiller.

With a sharp command he'd make 'em stand
   And deliver their hard-earned dust,
Then drink the bar dry of rum and rye,
   As a Klondike bully must.

Without coming to blows he would tweak the nose
   Of dangerous Dan McGrew,
And becoming bolder, throw over his shoulder
    The Lady that's known as Lou.

Oh, tough as steak was Yukon Jake—
   Hardboiled as a picnic egg.
He washed his shirt in the Klondike dirt,
   And drunk his rum by the keg.

In fear of their lives (or because of their wives)
   He was shunned by the best of his pals;
An outcast he, from the comraderie
   Of all but wild animals.

So he bought the whole of Shark Tooth Shoal,
   A reef in the Bering Sea,
And he lived by himself on a sea lion's shelf
   In lonely iniquity.

But miles away, in Keokuk, Ia.,
   Did a ruined maiden fight
To remove the smirch from the Baptist Church
   By bringing the heathen Light.

And the Elders declared that all would be squared
   If she carried the holy words
From her Keokuk home to the hell-town Nome
   To save those sinful birds.

So, two weeks later, she took a freighter,
    For the gold-cursed land near the Pole,
But Heaven ain't made for a lass that's betrayed—
    She was wrecked on Shark Tooth Shoal!

All hands were tossed in the sea and lost—
    All but the maiden Ruth,
Who swam to the edge of the sea lion's ledge
    Where abode the love of her youth.

He was hunting a seal for his evening meal
    (He handled a mean harpoon)
When he saw at his feet not something to eat,
    But a girl in a frozen swoon.

Whom he dragged to his lair by her dripping hair,
    And he rubbed her knees with gin.
To his surprise she opened her eyes
    And revealed—his Original Sin!

His eight months' beard grew stiff and weird
    And it felt like a chestnut burr,
And he swore by his gizzard—and the Arctic blizzard
    That he'd do right by her.

But the cold sweat froze on the end of her nose
    Till it gleamed like a Tecla pearl,
While her bright hair fell like a flame from hell
    Down the back of the grateful girl.

But a hopeless rake was Yukon Jake
    The Hermit of Shark Tooth Shoal!
And the dizzy maid he rebetrayed
    And wrecked her immortal soul!

Then he rowed her ashore with a broken oar,
    And he sold her to Dan McGrew
For a husky dog and a hot egg-nog—
    As rascals are wont to do.

Now ruthless Ruth is a maid uncouth
    With scarlet cheeks and lips,
And she sings rough songs to the drunken throngs
    That come from the sealing ships.

For a rouge-stained kiss from this infamous miss
    They will give a seal's sleek fur,
Or perhaps a sable, if they are able;
    It's much the same to her. . . .

Oh the North Countree is a hard countree,
    That mothers a bloody brood;
And its icy arms hold hidden charms
    For the greedy, the sinful and lewd.

And strong men rust from the gold and lust
    That sears the Northland soul,
But the wickedest born from the Pole to the Horn
    Is the Hermit of Shark Tooth Shoal!

                                        EDWARD E. PARAMORE, JR

Arizona Nature Myth

Up in the heavenly saloon
Sheriff sun and rustler moon
Gamble, stuck in the sheriff's mouth
The fag end of an afternoon.

There in the bad town of the sky
Sheriff, nervy, wonders why
He's let himself wander so far West
On his own; he looks with a smoky eye

At the rustler opposite turning white,
Lays down a king for Law, sits tight
Bluffing. On it that crooked moon
Plays an ace and shoots for the light.

Spurs, badge, and uniform red,
(It looks like blood, but he's shamming dead),
Down drops the marshal, and under cover
Crawls out dogwise, ducking his head

But Law that don't get its man ain't Law.
Next day, faster on the draw,
Sheriff creeping up from the other side,
Blazes his way in through the back door.

But moon's not there. He's ridden out on
A galloping phenomenon,
A wonder horse, quick as light.
Moon's left town. Moon's clean gone.

JAMES MICHIE

Hialmar

The firing ceased and like a wounded foe
The day bled out in crimson: wild and high
A far hyena sent his voice of woe
Tingling in faint hysteria through the sky.

Thick lay the fatal harvest of the fight
In the grey twilight when the newly-dead
Collect those brindled scavengers of night
Whose bloodshot eyes must candle them to bed.

The dead slept on: but one among them rose
Out of his trance, and turned a patient eye
To where like cankers in a burning rose,
Out of the fading scarlet of the sky,

Great birds, descending, settled on the stones:
He knew their errand and he knew how soon
The wolf must make a pulpit of his bones
To skirl his shrill hosannas to the moon.

Great adjutants came wheeling from the hills,
And chaplain crows with smug, self-righteous face,
And vultures bald and red about the gills
As any hearty colonel at the base.

All creatures that grow fat on beauty's wreck,
They ranged themselves expectant round the kill,
And like a shrivelled arm each raw, red neck
Lifted the rusty dagger of its bill.

Then to the largest of that bony tribe
'O merry bird,' he shouted, 'work your will,
I offer my clean body as a bribe
That when upon its flesh you've gorged your fill,

'You'll take my heart and bear it in your beak
To where my sweetheart combs her yellow hair
Beside the Vaal: and if she bids you speak
Tell her you come to represent me there.

'Flounce out your feathers in their sleekest trim,
Affect the brooding softness of the dove—
Yea, smile, thou skeleton so foul and grim,
As fits the bland ambassador of love!

'And tell her, when the nights are wearing late
And the grey moonlight smoulders on her hair,
To brood no more upon her ghostly mate
Nor on the phantom children she would bear.

'Tell her I fought as blindly as the rest,
That none of them had wronged me whom I killed,
And she may seek within some other breast
The promise that I leave her unfulfilled.

'I should have been too tired for love or mirth
Stung as I am, and sickened by the truth—
Old men have hunted beauty from the earth
Over the broken bodies of our youth!'

ROY CAMPBELL

Castaway

Struggle he would with the sea-waves' embracing,
Hours on days unclasping the crested limbs,
All action, repulsing the storm-troopers,
Baling out the invaders:
'*I must not die, that's what the book says,
Must keep afloat, and the rockets dry.*'

There were days, though, when he would lie still,
And these most dangerous days, when he lulled,
The ripples dallied about him, carolling,
And wind struck suddenly out of sleep:
'*I must not die, that's what the book says,
Must keep afloat, and the rockets dry.*'

And when the fresh water died in its barrel,
And the biscuits crumbled quite away,
White were the salt-caked corners of his eyes,
Softer than flesh the black stuff on his bones.
'*He must not die,*' that's what the book said,
Its white pages fingered by the wind.

JULIAN MITCHELL

The Wreckers' Prayer

(NEWFOUNDLAND)

Give us a wrack or two, Good Lard,
For winter in Tops'il Tickle bes hard,
Wid grey frost creepin' like mortal sin
And perishin' lack of bread in the bin.

A grand rich wrack, us do humbly pray,
Busted abroad at the break o' day
An' hove clear in 'crost Tops'il Reef,
Wid victuals an' gear to beguile our grief.

God of reefs an' tides an' sky,
Heed ye our need and hark to our cry!
Bread by the bag an' beef by the cask—
Ease for sore bellies bes all we ask.

One grand wrack—or maybe two?—
Wid gear an' victuals to see us through
'Til Spring starts up like the leap of day
An' the fish strike back into Tops'il Bay.

One rich wrack—for Thy hand bes strong!
A barque or a brig from up-along
Bemused by thy twisty tides, O Lard!
For winter in Tops'il Tickle bes hard.

Loud an' long will us sing yer praise,
Merciful Fadder, O Ancient of Days,
Master of fog, an' tide, an' reef!
Heave us a wrack to beguile our grief. Amen.

THEODORE GOODRIDGE ROBERTS

The Shooting Of Dan McGrew

A bunch of the boys were whooping it up in the Malamute
    saloon;
The kid that handles the music-box was hitting a jag-time
    tune;
Back of the bar, in a solo game, sat Dangerous Dan
    McGrew,
And watching his luck was his light-o'-love, the lady that's
    known as Lou.

When out of the night, which was fifty below, and into the
    din and the glare,
There stumbled a miner fresh from the creeks, dog-dirty
    and loaded for beer.
He looked like a man with a foot in the grave, and scarcely
    the strength of a louse,
Yet he tilted a poke of dust on the bar, and he called for
    drinks for the house.
There was none could place the stranger's face, though we
    searched ourselves for a clue;
But we drank his health, and the last to drink was Dangerous
    Dan McGrew.

There's men that somehow just grip your eyes, and hold
    them hard like a spell;
And such was he, and he looked to me like a man who had
    lived in hell;
With a face most hair, and the dreary stare of a dog whose
    day is done,
As he watered the green stuff in his glass, and the drops fell
    one by one.

Then I got to figgering who he was, and wondering what
    he'd do,
And I turned my head—and there watching him was the
    lady that's known as Lou.

His eyes went rubbering round the room, and he seemed in
    a kind of daze,
Till at last that old piano fell in the way of his wandering
    gaze.
The rag-time kid was having a drink; there was no one else
    on the stool,
So the stranger stumbles across the room, and flops down
    there like a fool.
In a buckskin shirt that was glazed with dirt he sat, and I
    saw him sway;
Then he clutched the keys with his talon hands—my God!
    but that man could play!

Were you ever out in the Great Alone, when the moon was
    awful clear,
And the icy mountains hemmed you in with a silence you
    most could *hear*;
With only the howl of a timber wolf, and you camped there
    in the cold,
A half-dead thing in a stark, dead world, clean made for the
    muck called gold;
While high overhead, green, yellow, and red, the North
    Lights swept in bars—
Then you've a hunch what the music meant— . . . hunger
    and night and the stars.

And hunger not of the belly kind, that's banished with
    bacon and beans;
But the gnawing hunger of lonely men for a home and all
    that it means;
For a fireside far from the cares that are, four walls and a
    roof above;
But oh! so cramful of cosy joy, and crowned with a woman's
    love;
A woman dearer than all the world, and true as Heaven is
    true—
(God! how ghastly she looks through her rouge,—
    the lady that's known as Lou.)

Then on a sudden the music changed, so soft that you
    scarce could hear;
But you felt that your life had been looted clean of all that
    it once held dear;
That someone had stolen the woman you loved; that her
    love was a devil's lie;
That your guts were gone, and the best for you was to crawl
    away and die.
'Twas the crowning cry of a heart's despair, and it thrilled
    you through and through—
'I guess I'll make it a spread misere,' said Dangerous Dan
    McGrew.

The music almost died away . . . then it burst like a pent-up
    flood;
And it seemed to say, 'Repay, repay,' and my eyes were
    blind with blood.

The thought came back of an ancient wrong, and it stung
  like a frozen lash,
And the lust awoke to kill, to kill . . . then the music
  stopped with a crash,

And the stranger turned, and his eyes they burned in a most
  peculiar way;
In a buckskin shirt that was glazed with dirt he sat, and I
  saw him sway;
Then his lips went in in a kind of grin, and he spoke, and
  his voice was calm;
And, 'Boys,' says he, 'you don't know me, and none of you
  care a damn;
But I want to state, and my words are straight, and I'll bet
  my poke they're true,
That one of you is a hound of hell . . . and that one is Dan
  McGrew.'

Then I ducked my head, and the lights went out, and two
  guns blazed in the dark;
And a woman screamed, and the lights went up, and two
  men lay stiff and stark;
Pitched on his head, and pumped full of lead, was Dangerous
  Dan McGrew,
While the man from the creeks lay clutched to the breast of
  the lady that's known as Lou.

These are the simple facts of the case, and I guess I ought
  to know;
They say that the stranger was crazed with 'hooch', and I'm
  not denying it's so.

I'm not so wise as the lawyer guys, but strictly between us
    two—
The woman that kissed him—and pinched his poke—was
    the lady that's known as Lou.

ROBERT SERVICE

Drought Year

That time of drought the embered air
burned to the roots of timber and grass.
The crackling lime-scrub would not bear
and Mooni Creek was sand that year.
The dingoes' cry was strange to hear.

I heard the dingoes cry
in the whipstick scrub on the Thirty-mile Dry.
I saw the wagtail take his fill
perching in the seething skull.
I saw the eel wither where he curled
in the last blood-drop of a spent world.

I heard the bone whisper in the hide
of the big red horse that lay where he died.
Prop that horse up, make him stand,
hoofs turned down in the bitter sand—
make him stand at the gate of the Thirty-mile Dry.
Turn this way and you will die—
and strange and loud was the dingoes' cry.

JUDITH WRIGHT

Flood Year

Walking up the driftwood beach at day's end
I saw it, thrust up out of a hillock of sand—
a frail bleached clench of fingers dried by wind—
the dead child's hand.

And they are mourning there still, though I forget,
the year of flood, the scoured ruined land,
the herds gone down the current, the farms drowned,
and the child never found.

When I was there the thick hurling waters
had gone back to the river, the farms were almost drained.
Banished half-dead cattle searched the dunes; it rained;
river and sea met with a wild sound.

Oh with a wild sound water flung into air
where sea met river; all the country round
no heart was quiet. I walked on the driftwood sand
and saw the pale crab crouched, and came to a stand
thinking, A child's hand. The child's hand.

JUDITH WRIGHT

Birkett's Eagle

Adam Birkett took his gun
    And climbed from Wasdale Head;
He swore he could spare no more lambs
    To keep an eagle fed.

So Birkett went along the Trod
   That climbs by Gavel Neese,
Till on his right stood Gavel Crag,
   And leftward fell the screes.

The mist whirled up from Ennerdale,
   And Gavel Crag grew dim,
And from the rocks on Birkett's right
   The eagle spoke to him.

'What ails you, Adam Birkett,
   That you have climbed so far
To make an end of Lucifer,
   That was the Morning Star?

'If there's a heaven, Birkett,
   There's certainly a hell;
And he who would kill Lucifer
   Destroys himself as well.'

The mist whirled off from Gavel Crag,
   And swept towards Beck Head,
And Adam Birkett took his aim
   And shot the eagle dead.

He looked down into Ennerdale
   To where its body fell,
And at his back stood Gavel Crag,
   And at his feet lay Hell.

Birkett scrambled off the rocks,
  And back on to the Trod,
And on his right lay Ennerdale,
  And on his left stood God.

What was it, Adam Birkett,
  That fell on to the scree?
For I feared it might be Lucifer,
  That once was dear to me.

'And from Carlisle to Ravenglass,
  From Shap to St Bees Head,
There's nobody worth vanquishing
  If Lucifer is dead.'

Birkett's dogs leapt all about
  As he came down the scree,
But he said, 'I have killed Lucifer,
  And what is left for me?'

Birkett's lambs leapt all about
  As he came off the fell,
But he said, 'I have killed Lucifer,
  And maybe God as well.'

But Lucifer the Morning Star
  Walked thoughtfully away
From the screes beyond the Gavel
  Where the eagle's body lay.

And as he went by Black Sail Pass
    And round below Kirk Fell,
He looked like young Tom Ritson
    Who knew the Birketts well.

And he came down to Wasdale Head,
    Young Ritson to the life,
With an apple in his pocket
    Which he gave to Birkett's wife.

DOROTHY S. HOWARD

The Dead Swagman

His rusted billy left beside the tree;
Under a root, most carefully tucked away,
His steel-rimmed glasses folded in their case
Of mildewed purple velvet; there he lies
In the sunny afternoon and takes his ease,
Curled like a possum within the hollow trunk.

He came one winter evening when the tree
Hunched its broad back against the rain, and made
His camp, and slept, and did not wake again.
Now white ants make a home within his skull:
His old friend Fire has walked across the hill
And blackened the old tree and the old man
And buried him half in ashes, where he lay.

It might be called a lonely death. The tree
Had its own alien life beneath the sun,
Yet both belong to the Bush, and now are one:
The roots and bones lie close among the soil,
And he ascends in leaves towards the sky.

NANCY CATO

Camp Fever

Camped by a creek and didn't speak for a week:
The continual bell of the smaller frogs, the croak
Of 'bulls' in the bulrushes, and the chirp
Of crickets in my bunk. He'd harp and harp
That fellow, on the weather, until, I tell you,
I, maddened, could but threaten, 'Very well, you—'
And, then, we two fell out, fell on each other,
And bitterly fought as brother fights with brother,
A bloody mess, the tent, and out he went,
His two lights out; fell into the river. Meant
To bathe his wounds; wound up instead
As posted missing in the flood. Poor dead
Cow, now, I miss him. Now I tramp the river
How I'd nurse him, to drag him out and shiver
Listening to his tales of weather, never
Again to quarrel, or pitch in peril of camp fever.

JOHN BLIGHT

Black Stockman

We talked about tobacco and the difficulties of getting it,
Quilp smoking an old black pipe,
Sucking at the ashes of ashes.
I gave him two cigarettes and his well-being broke into
    blossom
Just like a wrinkled old gum putting a white head
High into a stinging cloud of bees.
'This is good tobacco,' he said.

The horse's head dropped lower and lower,
Flies pitched on the lids of his closed eyes and walked
Bravely round the inside of the bit-ring and off
Onto the white-flecked lips. His tail hung thin,
Listless as a branch of leaves,
Paper bark leaves above a billabong.

And we talked about cattle; we talked . . . But I
Lived in long hiatus filled with a dreaming, seeing,
As eyes wandered, cows
Ankle-deep in black mud, reaching out
Long necks towards the soupy water, saw
The last limp leaves of dying lilies,
And a rotting blossom,

Talking to Quilp,
Talking to Quilp at the tail of a sleepy herd.

                                                    W. HART SMITH

The Devil In Texas

He scattered tarantulas over the roads,
Put thorns on the cactus and horns on the toads,
He sprinkled the sands with millions of ants
So the man who sits down must wear soles on his pants.
He lengthened the horns of the Texas steer,
And added an inch to the jack rabbit's ear;
He put mouths full of teeth in all of the lakes,
And under the rocks he put rattlesnakes.

He hung thorns and brambles on all of the trees,
He mixed up the dust with jiggers and fleas;
The rattlesnake bites you, the scorpion stings,
The mosquito delights you by buzzing his wings.
The heat in the summer's a hundred and ten,
Too hot for the Devil and too hot for men;
And all who remain in that climate soon bear
Cuts, bites, and stings, from their feet to their hair.

He quickened the buck of the bronco steed,
And poisoned the feet of the centipede;
The wild boar roams in the black chaparral;
It's a hell of a place that we've got for a hell.
He planted red pepper beside every brook;
The Mexicans use them in all that they cook.
Just dine with a Mexican, then you will shout,
'I've hell on the inside as well as the out!'

ANON.

On The Swag

His body doubled
    under the pack
    that sprawls untidily
    on his old back
    the cold wet deadbeat
    plods up the track.

The cook peers out:
    'Oh curse that old lag
    here again
    with his clumsy swag
    made of a dirty old
    turnip bag'.

'Bring him in cook
    from the grey level sleet
    put silk on his body
    slippers on his feet,
    give him fire
    and bread and meat

'Let the fruit be plucked
    and the cake be iced
    the bed be snug
    and the wine be spiced
    in the old cove's nightcap:
    for this is Christ.'

                                    R.A.K. MASON

THE EIGHT O'CLOCK WALK

Ballad Of The Long Drop

We dropped a chap that raped a child:
He gave no trouble, kind and mild.
We dropped a kid that killed a cop:
He made a lightish drop.

We dropped a well-fed man who bled
Old ladies—and the prayers he said!
We dropped a gangster who was bold
But shivered with the cold.

We dropped a gentlemanly rake
Who said it wasn't our mistake
We dropped a fool or two who tried
To struggle as they died.

We dropped a lad who killed by whim,
Who cursed us as we pinioned him.
We dropped a girl who shot a bloke
Because her heart was broke.

Her heart was broke. She did him in
For love: but love like hers is sin.
We dropped her, for we drop them straight
For love as well as hate.

For love as well as hate we serve
To break the neck and break the nerve
Of those who break the laws of man:
We serve you all as best we can.

JOHN PUDNEY

This Malefactor

This malefactor dies how many times a day,
With warders in fair play
With dominoes or rummy, draughts or whist.
Let's hope they give the rope a proper twist!

The brute who killed for passion, or for greed,
Now waits a colder deed,
Precisely done by one who is expert,
For Christ's sake is it easy, will it hurt?

This malefactor dies how many times a night,
Within a warder's sight.
And cons the details as he dreams and wakes.
What happens if this bloody rope-length breaks?

This brute, who killed but once, dies now again,
And often, without pain,
Until his neck is broken, dead on time.
Is it a fact they chuck you in quick-lime?

God give you Sunday patience till you die
Beneath a Tuesday sky!
May God have special mercy to endow!
God, in your mercy, can't you make it now?

JOHN PUDNEY

The Faking Boy

The faking boy to the trap is gone,
At the nubbing chit you'll find him;
The hempen cord they have girded on,
And his elbows pinned behind him.
'Smash my glim!' cries the reg'lar card,
'Though the girl you love betrays you,
Don't split, but die both game and hard,
And grateful pals shall praise you!'

The bolt it fell—a jerk, a strain!
The sheriffs fled asunder;
The faking boy ne'er spoke again,
For they pulled his legs from under.
And there he dangles on the tree,
That soul of love and bravery!
Oh, that such men should victims be
Of law, and law's vile knavery!

ANON.

The Culprit

The night my father got me
His mind was not on me;
He did not plague his fancy
To muse if I should be
The son you see.

The day my mother bore me
She was a fool and glad,
For all the pain I cost her,
That she had borne the lad
That borne she had.

My mother and my father
Out of the light they lie;
The warrant would not find them,
And here 'tis only I
Shall hang so high.

Oh let not man remember
The soul that God forgot,
But fetch the county kerchief
And noose me in the knot,
And I will rot.

For so the game is ended
That should not have begun.
My father and my mother
They had a likely son,
And I have none.

                                          A.E. HOUSMAN

Eight O'Clock

He stood, and heard the steeple sprinkle
The quarters on the morning town.
One, two, three, four, to market-place and people
It tossed them down.

Strapped, noosed, nighing his hour,
He stood and counted them and cursed his luck;
And then the clock collected in the tower
Its strength, and struck.

A.E. HOUSMAN

The Epitaph In Form Of A Ballad

Which Villon made for himself and his comrades, expecting to
to be hanged along with them

Men, brother men, that after us yet live,
   Let not your hearts too hard against us be;
For if some pity of us poor men ye give,
   The sooner God shall take of you pity.
   Here are we five or six strung up, you see,
And here the flesh that all too well we fed
Bit by bit eaten and rotten, and rent shred,
   And we the bones grow dust and ash withal;
Let no man laugh at us discomforted,
   But pray to God that he forgive us all.

If we call on you, brothers, to forgive,
   Ye should not hold our prayer in scorn, though **we**
Were slain by law; ye know that all alive
   Have not wit alway to walk righteously;
   Make therefore intercession heartily
With him that of a virgin's womb was bred,
That his grace be not as a dry well-head
   For us, nor let hell's thunder on us fall;
We are dead, let no man harry or vex us dead,
   But pray to God that he forgive us all.

The rain has washed and laundered us all five,
    And the sun dried and blackened; yea, perdie,
Ravens and pies with beaks that rend and rive
    Have dug our eyes out, and plucked off for fee
    Our beards and eyebrows; never are we free,
Not once, to rest; but here and there still sped,
Driven at its wild will by the wind's change led,
More pecked of birds than fruit on a garden-wall;
Men, for God's love, let no gibe here be said,
    But pray to God that he forgive us all.

Prince Jesus, that of all art lord and head,
Keep us, that hell be not our bitter bed;
    We have nought to do in such a master's hall.
Be not ye therefore of our fellowhead,
    But pray to God that he forgive us all.

FRANÇOIS VILLON
(TRANSLATED BY A. C. SWINBURNE)

Gallows Bird

He stares at his toes
Where ice makes him nails

It rolls down his thighs
The wind fills his nose

And the dust of his thought
Licks its vault

Bald, eyeless, caught,
He grins at his toes
Though ice makes him nails.
Is this the gross cut-throat?
With nods and smiles?

A vine catches his toes,
Nettles reach to his knees,
Honey slips from his teeth,
His head brims with bees,
Wax pads his eyes,
Rocking at ease
He hums to himself,
And the moss all the while
Is closing his eyes,
Is bearding his smile.

PETER REDGROVE

Invitation To The Dance

The condemned prisoner stirred, but could not stir:
Cold had shackled the blood-prints of the knout.
The light of his death's dawn put the dark out.
He lay, his lips numb to the frozen floor.
He dreamed some other prisoner was dragged out—
Nightmare of command in the dawn, and a shot.
The bestial gaoler's boot was at his ear.

Upon his sinews torturers had grown strong,
The inquisitor, old against a tongue that could not,
Being torn out, plead even for death.

All bones were shattered, the whole body unstrung.
Horses, plunging apart towards North and South,
Tore his heart up by the shrieking root.
He was flung to the blow-fly and the dog's fang.

Pitched onto his mouth in a black ditch
All spring he heard the lovers rustle and sigh.
The sun stank. Rats worked at him secretly.
Rot and maggot stripped him stitch by stitch.
Yet still this dream engaged his vanity:
That could he get upright he would dance and cry
Shame on every shy or idle wretch.

                                                    TED HUGHES

A Shropshire Lad

On moonlit heath and lonesome bank
  The sheep beside me graze;
And yon the gallows used to clank
  Fast by the four cross ways.

A careless shepherd once would keep
  The flocks by moonlight there,[1]
And high amongst the glimmering sheep
  The dead man stood on air.

They hang us now in Shrewsbury jail;
  The whistles blow forlorn,
And trains all night groan on the rail
  To men that die at morn.

[1] Hanging in chains was called keeping sheep by moonlight

There sleeps in Shrewsbury jail tonight,
  Or wakes, as may betide,
A better lad, if things went right,
  Than most that sleep outside.

And naked to the hangman's noose
  The morning clocks will ring
A neck God made for other use
  Than strangling in a string.

And sharp the link of life will snap,
  And dead on air will stand
Heels that held up as straight a chap
  As treads upon the land.

So here I'll watch the night and wait
  To see the morning shine,
When he will hear the stroke of eight
  And not the stroke of nine;

And wish my friend as sound a sleep
  As lads' I did not know,
That shepherded the moonlit sheep
  A hundred years ago.

                              A.E. HOUSMAN

The Carpenter's Son

'Here the hangman stops his cart:
Now the best of friends must part.
Fare you well, for ill fare I:
Live, lads, and I will die.

'Oh, at home had I but stayed
'Prenticed to my father's trade,
Had I stuck to plane and adze,
I had not been lost, my lads.

'Then I might have built perhaps
Gallows-trees for other chaps,
Never dangled on my own,
Had I but left ill alone.

'Now, you see, they hang me high,
And the people passing by
Stop to shake their fists and curse;
So 'tis come from ill to worse.

'Here hang I, and right and left
Two poor fellows hang for theft:
All the same's the luck we prove,
Though the midmost hangs for love.

'Comrades all, that stand and gaze,
Walk henceforth in other ways;
See my neck and save your own:
Comrades all, leave ill alone.

'Make some day a decent end,
Shrewder fellows than your friend.
Fare you well, for ill fare I:
Live, lads, and I will die.'

A.E. HOUSMAN

Two Poems

(AFTER A.E. HOUSMAN)

1.

What, still alive at twenty-two,
A clean upstanding chap like you?
Sure, if your throat 'tis hard to slit,
Slit your girl's, and swing for it.

Like enough, you won't be glad,
When they come to hang you, lad;
But bacon's not the only thing
That's cured by hanging from a string.

So, when the spilt ink of the night
Spreads o'er the blotting pad of light,
Lads whose job is still to do
Shall whet their knives, and think of you.

2.

'Tis Summer Time on Bredon,
    And now the farmers swear;
The cattle rise and listen
    In valleys far and near,
    And blush at what they hear.

But when the mists in autumn
    On Bredon tops are thick,
The happy hymns of farmers
    Go up from fold and rick,
    The cattle then are sick.

HUGH KINGSMILL

Danny Deever

'What are the bugles blowin' for?' said Files-on-Parade.
'To turn you out, to turn you out,' the Colour-Sergeant
    said.
'What makes you look so white, so white?' said Files-on-
    Parade.
'I'm dreadin' what I've got to watch,' the Colour-
    Sergeant said.
    For they're hangin' Danny Deever, you can hear the
        Dead March play,
    The regiment's in 'ollow square—they're hangin' him
        today;
    They've taken of his buttons off an' cut his stripes away,
    An' they're hangin' Danny Deever in the mornin'.

'What makes the rear-rank breathe so 'ard?' said Files-on-
    Parade.
'It's bitter cold, it's bitter cold,' the Colour-Sergeant said.
'What makes that front-rank man fall down?' says Files-on-
    Parade.
'A touch o' sun, a touch o' sun,' the Colour-Sergeant said.
    They are hangin' Danny Deever, they are marching of 'im
        round,
    They 'ave 'alted Danny Deever by 'is coffin on the
        ground;
    An' 'e'll swing in 'arf a minute for a sneakin' shootin'
        hound—
    O they're hangin' Danny Deever in the mornin'.

''Is cot was right-'and cot to mine,' said Files-on-Parade.
''E's sleepin' out and far tonight,' the Colour-Sergeant said.

'I've drunk 'is beer a score o' times,' said Files-on-Parade.
''E's drinkin' bitter beer alone,' the Colour-Sergeant said.
  They are hangin' Danny Deever, you must mark 'im to
      'is place,
  For 'e shot a comrade sleepin'—you must look 'im in
      the face;
  Nine 'undred of the county an' 'is regiment's disgrace,
  While they're hangin' Danny Deever in the mornin'.

'What's that so black agin the sun?' said Files-on-Parade.
'It's Danny fightin' 'ard for life,' the Colour-Sergeant said.
'What's that that whimpers over'ead?' said Files-on-Parade.
'It's Danny's soul that's passin' now,' the Colour-Sergeant
  said.
  For they're done with Danny Deever, you can 'ear the
      quickstep play,
  The regiment's in column, an' they're marchin' us away;
  Ho! the young recruits are shakin' an' they'll want their
      beer today
  After hangin' Danny Deever in the mornin'.

                      RUDYARD KIPLING

Clever Tom Clinch

GOING TO BE HANGED, 1727

As clever Tom Clinch, while the rabble was bawling,
Rode stately through Holborn to die in his calling,
He stopt at the George for a bottle of sack,
And promised to pay for it when he came back.

His waistcoat, and stockings, and breeches, were white;
His cap had a new cherry ribbon to tie't.
The maids to the doors and the balconies ran,
And said, 'Lack-a-day, he's a proper young man!'
But, as from the windows the ladies he spied,
Like a beau in the box, he bow'd low on each side!
And when his last speech the loud hawkers did cry,
He swore from his cart, 'It was all a damn'd lie!'
The hangman for pardon fell down on his knee;
Tom gave him a kick in the guts for his fee:
Then said, 'I must speak to the people a little;
But I'll see you all damn'd before I will whittle.
My honest friend Wild (may he long hold his place)
He lengthen'd my life with a whole year of grace.
Take courage, dear comrades, and be not afraid,
Nor slip this occasion to follow your trade;
My conscience is clear, and my spirits are calm,
And thus I go off, without prayer-book or psalm;
Then follow the practice of clever Tom Clinch,
Who hung like a hero, and never would flinch.'

JONATHAN SWIFT

SNAKES AND THINGS

In The Snake Park

A white-hot midday in the Snake Park.
Lethargy lay here and there in coils,
And here and there a neat obsidian head
Lay dreaming on a plaited pillow of its own
Loops like a pretzel or a true-love-knot.

A giant Python seemed a heap of tyres;
Two Nielsen's Vipers looked for a way out,
Sick of their cage and one another's curves;
And the long Ringsnake brought from Lembuland
Poured slowly through an opening like smoke.

Leaning intently forward a young girl
Discerned in stagnant water on a rock
A dark brown shoestring or discarded whiplash,
Then read the label to find out the name,
Then stared again: it moved. She screamed.

Old Pier Vander leant with us that day
On the low wall around the rocky space
Where amid broken quartz that cast no shade
Snakes twitched or slithered, or appeared to sleep,
Or lay invisible in the singing glare.

The sun throbbed like a fever as he spoke:
'Look carefully at this shrub with glossy leaves.'
Leaves bright as brass. 'That leaf on top
Just there, do you see that it has eyes?
That's a Green Mamba, and it's watching *you*.

'A man I once knew did survive the bite,
Saved by a doctor running with a knife,
Serum and all. He was never the same again.
Vomiting blackness, agonizing, passing blood,
Part paralysed, near gone, he felt

'(He told me later) he would burst apart;
But the worst agony was in his mind—
Unbearable nightmare, worse than total grief
Or final loss of hope, impossibly magnified
To a blind passion of panic and extreme distress.'

'Why should that little head have power
To inject all horror for no reason at all?'
'Ask me another—and beware of snakes.'
The sun was like a burning glass. Face down
The girl who screamed had fallen in a faint.

WILLIAM PLOMER

Snakecharmer

As the gods began one world, and man another,
So the snakecharmer begins a snaky sphere
With moon-eye, mouth-pipe. He pipes. Pipes green. Pipes
   water.

Pipes water green until green waters waver
With reedy lengths and necks and undulatings.
And as his notes twine green, the green river

Shapes its images around his songs.
He pipes a place to stand on, but no rocks,
No floor: a wave of flickering grass-tongues

Supports his foot. He pipes a world of snakes,
Of sways and coilings, from the snake-rooted bottom
Of his mind. And now nothing but snakes

Is visible. The snake-scales have become
Leaf, become eyelid; snake-bodies, bough, breast
Of tree and human. And he within this snakedom

Rules the writhings which make manifest
His snakehood and his might with pliant tunes
From his thin pipe. Out of this green nest

As out of eden's navel twist the lines
Of snaky generations: let there be snakes!
And snakes there were, are, will be—till yawns

Consume this piper and he tires of music
And pipes the world back to the simple fabric
Of snake-warp, snake weft. Pipes the cloth of snakes

To a melting of green waters, till no snake
Shows its head, and those green waters back to
Water, to green, to nothing like a snake.
Puts up his pipe and lids his moony eye.

                                        SYLVIA PLATH

Burning The Cat

In the spring, by the big shuck-pile
Between the bramble-choked brook where the copper-
    heads
Curled in the first sun, and the mud road,
All at once it could no longer be ignored.
The season steamed with an odour for which
There has never been a name, but it shouted above all.
When I went near, the wood-lice were in its eyes
And a nest of beetles in the white fur of its arm-pit.
I built a fire there by the shuck-pile
But it did no more than pop the beetles
And singe the damp fur, raising a stench
Of burning hair that bit through the sweet day-smell.
Then thinking how time leches after indecency,
Since both grief is indecent and the lack of it,
I went away and fetched newspaper,
And wrapped it in dead events, days and days,
Soaked it in kerosene and put it in
With the garbage on a heaped nest of sticks;
It was harder to burn than the peels of oranges,
Bubbling and spitting, and the reek was like
Rank cooking that drifted with the smoke out
Through the budding woods and clouded the shining
    dogwood.
But I became stubborn: I would consume it
Though the pyre should take me a day to build
And the flames rise over the house. And hours I fed
That burning, till I was black and streaked with sweat;
And poked it out then, with charred meat still clustering
Thick around the bones. And buried it so

As I could have done in the first place, for
The earth is slow, but deep, and good for hiding;
I would have used it if I had understood
How nine lives can vanish in one flash of a dog's jaws,
A car or a copperhead, and yet how one small
Death, however reckoned, is hard to dispose of.

W.S. MERWIN

The Barge Horse

The brasses jangle and the hausers tighten:
look how this huge-limbed beauty leans and strains
against the harness, that proud arch of neck
curved hard and low with labour, the round lines
all taut with tension. And the snub barge
wallowing after through the weeds and lilies
in the brown water of the long canal,
its broad beam heaving from the smoking shallows.

Haul, O haul, my lovely, lively horse.
Fire leaps from under the iron of your hoof,
your straight stiff foreleg tight with sinew now.
Even your masters, men, rehearse
this drag of labour on their own behalf,
their barges built from fear you never know.

SEAN JENNETT

The Bull Moses

A hoist up and I could lean over
The upper edge of the high half-door,
My left foot ledged on the hinge, and look in at the byre's
Blaze of darkness: a sudden shut-eyed look
Backward into the head.
                                    Blackness is depth
Beyond star, but the warm weight of his breathing,
The ammoniac reek of his litter, the hotly-tongued
Mash of his cud, steamed against me.
Then, slowly, as on to the mind's eye—
The brow like masonry, the deep-keeled neck:
Something come up there onto the brink of the gulf,
Hadn't heard of the world, too deep in itself to be called
    to,
Stood in sleep. He would swing his muzzle at a fly
But the square of sky where I hung, shouting, waving,
Was nothing to him; nothing of our light
Found any reflection in him.
                                    Each dusk the farmer led him
Down to the pond to drink, and smell the air,
And he took no pace but the farmer
Led him to take it; as if he knew nothing
Of the ages and continents of his fathers,
Shut, while he wombed, to a dark shed
And steps between his door and the duckpond;
The weight of the sun and the moon and the world
    hammered
To a ring of brass through his nostrils.
                                    He would raise
His streaming muzzle and look out over the meadows,

But the grasses whispered nothing awake, the fetch
Of the distance drew nothing to momentum
In the locked black of his powers. He came strolling
   gently back,
Paused neither toward the pig-pens on his right,
Nor toward the cow-byres on his left: something
Deliberate in his leisure, some beheld future
Founding in his quiet.
                  I kept the door wide.
Closed it after him and pushed the bolt.

                        TED HUGHES

Death Of A Whale

When the mouse died, there was a sort of pity;
The tiny, delicate creature made for grief.
Yesterday, instead, the dead whale on the reef
Drew an excited multitude to the jetty.
How must a whale die to wring a tear?
Lugubrious death of a whale; the big
Feast for the gulls and sharks; the tug
Of the tide simulating life still there,
Until the air, polluted, swings this way
Like a door ajar from a slaughter-house.
Pooh! Pooh! spare us, give us the death of a mouse
By its tiny hole; not this in our lovely bay.
Sorry, we are, too, when a child dies:
But at the immolation of a race, who cries?

                        JOHN BLIGHT

The Bull Calf

The thing could barely stand. Yet taken
from his mother and the barn smells
he still impressed with his pride,
with the promise of sovereignty in the way
his head moved to take us in.
The fierce sunlight tugging the maize from the ground
licked at his shapely flanks.
He was too young for all that pride.
I thought of the deposed Richard II.

'No money in bull calves,' Freeman had said.
The visiting clergyman rubbed the nostrils
now snuffing pathetically at the windless day.
'A pity,' he sighed.
My gaze slipped off his hat toward the empty sky
that circled over the black knot of men,
over us and the calf waiting for the first blow.

Struck,
the bull calf drew in his thin forelegs
as if gathering strength for a mad rush . . .
tottered . . . raised his darkening eyes to us,
and I saw we were at the far end
of his frightened look, growing smaller and smaller
till we were only the ponderous mallet
that flicked his bleeding ear
and pushed him over on his side, stiffly,
like a block of wood.

Below the hill's crest
the river snuffled on the impoverished beach.
We dug a deep pit and threw the dead calf into it.
It made a wet sound, a sepulchral gurgle,
as the warm sides bulged and flattened.
Settled, the bull calf lay as if asleep,
one foreleg over the other,
bereft of pride and so beautiful now,
without movement, perfectly still in the cool pit,
I turned away and wept.

IRVING LAYTON

Song

Old Adam, the carrion crow,
The old crow of Cairo;
He sat in the shower, and let it flow
Under his tail and over his crest;
And through every feather
Leaked the wet weather;
And the bough swung under his nest;
For his beak it was heavy with marrow.
Is that the wind dying? O no;
It's only two devils, that blow
Through a murderer's bones, to and fro,
In the ghosts' moonshine.

Ho! Eve, my grey carrion wife,
When we have supped on kings' marrow
Where shall we drink and make merry our life?

Our nest it is Queen Cleopatra's skull,
'Tis cloven and cracked,
And battered and hacked,
But with tears of blue eyes it is full:
Let us drink then, my raven of Cairo.
Is that the wind dying? O no;
It's only two devils, that blow
Through a murderer's bones, to and fro,
In the ghosts' moonshine.

GEORGE DARLEY

A London Sparrow's If

If you c'n keep alive when li'l bleeders
    Come arter y' wi' catapults an' stones;
If you c'n grow up unpertickler feeders,
    An' live on rubbidge, crumbs, an' 'addock bones;
If you c'n nest up in the bloomin' gutters,
    An' dodge the blinkin' tabby on the tiles;
Nip under wheels an' never get the flutters,
    Wear brahn an' no bright-coloured fevver-styles;
If you ain't blown b' nippers (Cor, I'd skin 'em!);
    Stop in y'r shells nah, warm-like, under me;
Yours is the eggs an' everyfink 'at's in 'em—
    An' when they 'atch, your be cock-sparrers, see?

J.A. LINDON

The Mother

Between the legs
Of the sailors and whores
The cat walks
With a swollen belly of kittens

Be careful, kitty,
Their boots are sharp,
And they have too little love
For even their own kind.

RAYMOND SOUSTER

I—The Soldiers

Vergissmeinicht[1]

Three weeks gone and the combatants gone,
returning over the nightmare ground
we found the place again, and found
the soldier sprawling in the sun.

The frowning barrel of his gun
overshadowing. As we came on
that day, he hit my tank with one
like the entry of a demon.

Look. Here in the gunpit spoil
the dishonoured picture of his girl
who has put: *Steffi. Vergissmeinicht*
in a copybook gothic script.

We see him almost with content
abased, and seeming to have paid
and mocked at by his own equipment
that's hard and good when he's decayed.

But she would weep to see today
how on his skin the swart flies move;
and dust upon the paper eye
and the burst stomach like a cave.

[1] Forget me not

139

For here the lover and killer are mingled
who had one body and one heart.
And death who had the soldier singled
has done the lover mortal hurt.

KEITH DOUGLAS

Reconciliation

All day beside the shattered tank he'd lain
Like a limp creature hacked out of its shell,
Now shrivelling on the desert's grid,
Now floating above a sharp-set ridge of pain.

There came a roar, like water, in his ear.
The mortal dust was laid. He seemed to be lying
In a cool coffin of stone walls,
While memory slid towards a plunging weir.

The time that was, the time that might have been
Find in this shell of stone a chance to kiss
Before they part eternally:
He feels a world without, a world within

Wrestle like old antagonists, until each is
Balancing each. Then, in a heavenly calm,
The lock gates open, and beyond
Appear the argent, swan-assemblied reaches.

C. DAY LEWIS

'They'

The Bishop tells us: 'When the boys come back
They will not be the same; for they'll have fought
In a just cause: they lead the last attack
On Anti-Christ; their comrades' blood has bought
New right to breed an honourable race,
They have challenged Death and dared him face to face.'

'We're none of us the same!' the boys reply.
'For George lost both his legs; and Bill's stone blind;
Poor Jim's shot through the lungs and like to die;
And Bert's gone syphilitic: you'll not find
A chap who's served that hasn't found *some* change.'
And the Bishop said: 'The ways of God are strange!'

SIEGFRIED SASSOON

The Dream

Floating in file across a glassy waste of sand
They came to me: Arm, Leg, and Hand.
Before the watching mind they halted and
Arm wagged roguish finger, giggled, said:
'I am from Private Smith he isn't dead
But boxer once he can't box now.'

And chuckled. So, in turn, came Leg,
Slid up, spun toppling like a peg,
And sniggered: 'From Private Jones I beg
to state he was an athlete he's not in pain
but he doesn't know yet that he won't run again
in running shoes hear cheers he can't run now.'

Then, rude-gesturing, came Hand:
'See these,' he crowed and fingers fanned:
'From Private Brown as pianist all the land
knew him what now? left handed tricks
popular performer at the flicks
why not? but only half a pianist now.'

And giggling they glided off, Arm, Leg, and Hand;
And as they went they chuckled and
Their laughter grew until the sand
Was filled and swirled by dark, wild, sobbing mirth
At what men do to men upon this earth.
And a thin cry died: 'How long, Lord? How. . . .'

                                    MUNGO B. MACCALLUM

Postscript

You won't even die like a dog.
Most of the dogs I've seen died fast and clean
With their guts spread on the pavement in a neat little
    pile,
But you'll die unlovely and have a lot of time
To think about it, some time before you can't
Spit out all the blood coming from your stomach
And you choke to death on it, but it was your own
Good red blood and it was a colourful way (joke) to kick
    the bucket.

But the biggest trouble is the worms
Don't know the score, they didn't have their radios tuned
   in
When the pot-belly boys were shouting to the wide wide
   world
The sweet little lowdown on life, liberty, and the pursuit
   of virgins,
So the little crawlers don't know a thing, they get
   hungry and anything they see
They eat because they can't stand starving to death,
   strange as it seems;

And all those bodies lying there going nowhere fast
Look mighty good to the little devils, and out they come
On their bellies in open order
And get crackin'.

Too bad they don't know any better.

RAYMOND SOUSTER

Schwere Gustav

Schwere Gustav, built by Krupps,
Was the largest of all guns:
Of thirty-one-inch calibre,
It fired a shell of seven tons.

Worked by fifteen hundred troops
Topped by a general, no less,
Gustav fired two rounds a day,
But after sixty was U.S.

The soldiers seeing Gustav's barrel
Huge against the eastern sky,
And his complicated breech,
Knew why they had got to die.

Accumulated capital
Made possible this symbol of
Our deep, ridiculous desires.
O war, O Gustav and O love!

ROY FULLER

The Execution Of Cornelius Vane

*Le combat spirituel est aussi brutal que la bataille
d'hommes; mais la vision de la justice est le plaisir de
Dieu seul.*—Arthur Rimbaud

Arraigned before his worldly gods
He would have said:
'I, Cornelius Vane,
A fly in the sticky web of life,
Shot away my right index finger.
I was alone, on sentry, in the chill twilight after dawn,
And the act cost me a bloody sweat.
Otherwise the cost was trivial—they had no evidence,
And I lied to the wooden fools who tried me.
When I returned from hospital
They made me a company cook:
I peel potatoes and other men fight.'

For nearly a year Cornelius peeled potatoes
And his life was full of serenity.
Then the enemy broke our line
And their hosts spread over the plains
Like unleashed beads.
Every man was taken—
Shoemakers, storemen, grooms—
And arms were given them
That they might stem the oncoming host.

Cornelius held out his fingerless hand
And remarked that he couldn't shoot.
'But you can stab,' the sergeant said,
So he fell in with rest, and, a little group,
They marched away towards the enemy.

After an hour they halted for a rest.
They were already in the fringe of the fight:
Desultory shells fell about them,
And past them retreating gunteams
Galloped in haste.
But they must go on.

Wounded stragglers came down the road,
Haggard and limping
Their arms and equipment tossed away.
Cornelius Vane saw them, and his heart was beating
    wildly,
For he must go on.

At the next halt
He went aside to piss,
And whilst away a black shell
Burst near him:
Hot metal shrieked past his face;
Bricks and earth descended like hail,
And the acrid stench of explosive filled his nostrils.

Cornelius pitched his body to the ground
And crouched in trembling fear.
Another shell came singing overhead,
Nowhere near.

But Cornelius sprang to his feet, his pale face set.
He willed nothing, saw nothing, only before him
Were the free open fields:
To the fields he ran.

He was still running when he began to perceive
The tranquillity of the fields
And the battle distant.
Away in the north-east were men marching on a road;
Behind were the smoke-puffs of shrapnel,
And in the west the sun declining
In a sky of limpid gold.

When night came finally
He had reached a wood.
In the thickness of the trees
The cold wind was excluded,
And here he slept a few hours

In the early dawn
The chill mist and heavy dew
Pierced his bones and wakened him.
There was no sound of battle to be heard.

In the open fields again
The sun shone sickly through the mist.
And the dew was icy to the feet.
So Cornelius ran about in that white night,
The sun's wan glare his only guide.

Coming to a canal
He ran up and down like a dog
Deliberating where to cross.
One way he saw a bridge
Loom vaguely, but approaching
He heard voices and turned about.
He went far the other way,
But growing tired before he found a crossing,
Plunged into the icy water and swam.
The water gripped with agony;
His clothes sucked the heavy water,
And as he ran again
Water oozed and squelched from his boots,
His coat dripped and his teeth chattered.

He came to a farm.
Approaching cautiously, he found it deserted.
Within he discarded his sopping uniform, dried himself
    and donned
Mufti he found in a cupboard.

Dark mouldy bread and bottled cider he also found
And was refreshed.
Whilst he was eating,
Suddenly,
Machine-guns opened fire not far away,
And their harsh throbbing
Darkened his soul with fear.

The sun was more golden now,
And as he went—
Always going west—
The mist grew thin.
About noon,
As he skirted the length of a wood
The warmth had triumphed and the spring day was
    beautiful.
Cornelius perceived with a new joy
Pale anemones and violets of the wood,
And wished that he might ever
Exist in the perception of these woodland flowers
And the shafts of yellow light that pierced
The green dusk.

Two days later
He entered a village and was arrested.
He was hungry, and the peace of the fields
Dissipated the terror that had been the strength of his will.

He was charged with desertion
And eventually tried by court-martial.
The evidence was heavy against him,
And he was mute in his own defence.

A dumb anger and a despair
Filled his soul.

He was found guilty.
Sentence: To suffer death by being shot.

The sentence duly confirmed,
One morning at dawn they led him forth.

He saw a party of his own regiment,
With rifles, looking very sad.
The morning was bright, and as they tied
The cloth over his eyes, he said to the assembly:
'What wrong have I done that I should leave these:
The bright sun rising
And the birds that sing?'

HERBERT READ

Sergeant-Major Money
(1917)

It wasn't our battalion, but we lay alongside it,
   So the story is as true as the telling is frank.
They hadn't one Line-officer left, after Arras,
   Except a batty major and the Colonel, who drank.

'B' Company Commander was fresh from the Depot,
   An expert on gas drill, otherwise a dud;
So Sergeant-Major Money carried on, as instructed,
   And that's where the swaddies began to sweat blood.

His Old Army humour was so well-spiced and hearty
   That one poor sod shot himself, and one lost his wits;
But discipline's maintained, and back in rest-billets
    The Colonel congratulates 'B' company on their kits.

The subalterns went easy, as was only natural
   With a terror like Money driving the machine,
Till finally two Welshmen, butties from the Rhondda,
   Bayoneted their bugbear in a field-canteen.

Well, we couldn't blame the officers, they relied on Money;
   We couldn't blame the pitboys, their courage was grand;
Or, least of all, blame Money, an old stiff surviving
   In a New (bloody) Army he couldn't understand.

ROBERT GRAVES

Bayonet Charge

Suddenly he awoke and was running—raw
In raw-seamed hot khaki, his sweat heavy,
Stumbling across a field of clods towards a green hedge
That dazzled with rifle fire, hearing
Bullets smacking the belly out of the air—
He lugged a rifle numb as a smashed arm;
The patriotic tear that had brimmed in his eye
Sweating like molten iron from the centre of his chest,—

In bewilderment then he almost stopped—
In what cold clockwork of the stars and the nations
Was he the hand pointing that second? He was running

Like a man who has jumped up in the dark and runs
Listening between his footfalls for the reason
Of his still running, and his foot hung like
Statuary in mid-stride. Then the shot-slashed furrows

Threw up a yellow hare that rolled like a flame
And crawled in a threshing circle, its mouth wide
Open silent, its eyes standing out.
He plunged past with his bayonet toward the green hedge,
King, honour, human dignity, etcetera
Dropped like luxuries in a yelling alarm
To get out of that blue crackling air
His terror's touchy dynamite.

TED HUGHES

Grenadier

The Queen she sent to look for me,
The sergeant he did say,
'Young man, a soldier will you be
For thirteen pence a day?'

For thirteen pence a day did I
Take off the things I wore,
And I have marched to where I lie,
And I shall march no more.

My mouth is dry, my shirt is wet,
My blood runs all away,
So now I shall not die in debt
For thirteen pence a day.

Tomorrow after new young men
The sergeant he must see,
For things will be all over then
Between the Queen and me.

And I shall have to bate my price,
For in the grave, they say,
Is neither knowledge nor device
Nor thirteen pence a day.

A.E. HOUSMAN

Counter-Attack

We'd gained our first objective hours before
While dawn broke like a face with blinking eyes,
Pallid, unshaved and thirsty, blind with smoke.
Things seemed all right at first. We held their line,
With bombers posted, Lewis guns well placed,
And clink of shovels deepening the shallow trench.
  The place was rotten with dead; green clumsy legs
  High-booted, sprawled and grovelled along the saps,
  And trunks, face downward, in the sucking mud,
  Wallowed like trodden sand-bags loosely filled;
  And naked sodden buttocks, mats of hair,
  Bulged, clotted heads slept in the plastering slime.
  And then the rain began—the jolly old rain!

A yawning soldier knelt against the bank,
Staring across the morning blear with fog;
He wondered when the Allemands would get busy;
And then, of course, they started with five-nines
Traversing, sure as fate, and never a dud.

Mute in the clamour of shells he watched them burst
Spouting dark earth and wire with gusts from hell,
While posturing giants dissolved in drifts of smoke.
He crouched and flinched, dizzy with galloping fear,
Sick for escape—loathing the strangled horror
And butchered, frantic gestures of the dead.

An officer came blundering down the trench:
'Stand-to and man the fire-step!' On he went . . .
Gasping and bawling, 'Fire-step . . . counter-attack!'
   Then the haze lifted. Bombing on the right
   Down the old sap: machine-guns on the left;
   And stumbling figures looming out in front.
   'O Christ, they're coming at us!' Bullets spat,
And he remembered his rifle . . . rapid fire . . .
And started blazing wildly . . . then a bang
Crumpled and spun him sideways, knocked him out
To grunt and wriggle: none heeded him; he choked
And fought the flapping veils of smothering gloom,
Lost in a blurred confusion of yells and groans . . .
Down, and down, and down, he sank and drowned,
Bleeding to death. The counter-attack had failed.

SIEGFRIED SASSOON

Wirers

'Pass it along, the wiring party's going out'—
And yawning sentries mumble, 'Wirers going out.'
Unravelling; twisting; hammering stakes with muffled thud,
They toil with stealthy haste and anger in their blood.

The Boche sends up a flare. Black forms stand rigid there,
Stock-still like posts; then darkness, and the clumsy ghosts
Stride hither and thither, whispering, tripped by
     clutching snare
Of snags and tangles.
                    Ghastly dawn with vaporous coasts
Gleams desolate along the sky, night's misery ended.

Young Hughes was badly hit; I heard him carried away,
Moaning at every lurch; no doubt he'll die today.
But *we* can say the front-line wire's been safely mended.

SIEGFRIED SASSOON

Attack

At dawn the ridge emerges massed and dun
In the wild purple of the glow'ring sun,
Smouldering through spouts of drifting smoke that
     shroud
The menacing scarred slope; and, one by one,
Tanks creep and topple forward to the wire.
The barrage roars and lifts. Then, clumsily bowed
With bombs and guns and shovels and battle-gear,
Men jostle and climb to meet the bristling fire.
Lines of grey, muttering faces, masked with fear,
They leave their trenches, going over the top,
While time ticks blank and busy on their wrists,
And hope, with furtive eyes and grappling fists,
Flounders in mud. O Jesus, make it stop!

SIEGFRIED SASSOON

Memorial Tablet

(GREAT WAR)

Squire nagged and bullied till I went to fight,
(Under Lord Derby's Scheme). I died in hell—
(They called it Passchendaele). My wound was slight,
And I was hobbling back; and then a shell
Burst slick upon the duck-boards: so I fell
Into the bottomless mud, and lost the light.

At sermon-time, while Squire is in his pew,
He gives my gilded name a thoughtful stare;
For, though low down upon the list, I'm there;
'*In proud and glorious memory*' . . . that's my due.
Two bleeding years I fought in France, for Squire:
I suffered anguish that he's never guessed.
Once I came home on leave: and then went west . . .
What greater glory could a man desire?

SIEGFRIED SASSOON

Dulce et Decorum Est

Bent double, like old beggars under sacks,
Knock-kneed, coughing like hags, we cursed through
    sludge,
Till on the haunting flares we turned our backs,
And towards our distant rest began to trudge.
Men marched asleep. Many had lost their boots,
But limped on, blood-shod. All went lame, all blind;
Drunk with fatigue; deaf even to the hoots
Of gas-shells dropping softly behind.

Gas! GAS! Quick, boys—An ecstasy of fumbling,
Fitting the clumsy helmets just in time,
But someone still was yelling out and stumbling
And floundering like a man in fire or lime.—
Dim through the misty panes and thick green light,
As under a green sea, I saw him drowning.

In all my dreams before my helpless sight
He plunges at me, guttering, choking, drowning.

If in some smothering dreams, you too could pace
Behind the waggon that we flung him in,
And watch the white eyes writhing in his face,
His hanging face, like a devil's sick of sin;
If you could hear, at every jolt, the blood
Come gargling from the froth-corrupted lungs,
Bitter as the cud
Of vile, incurable sores on innocent tongues,—
My friend, you would not tell with such high zest
To children ardent for some desperate glory,
The old Lie: Dulce et decorum est
Pro patria mori.

                                         WILFRED OWEN

II—The Sailors

Song Of The Dying Gunner A.A.1

Oh mother my mouth is full of stars
As cartridges in the tray
My blood is a twin-branched scarlet tree
And it runs all runs away.

Oh *Cooks to the Galley* is sounded off
And the lads are down in the mess
But I lie done by the forrard gun
With a bullet in my breast.

Don't send me a parcel at Christmas time
Of socks and nutty and wine
And don't depend on a long weekend
By the Great Western Railway line.

Farewell, Aggie Weston, the Barracks at Guz,
Hang my tiddley suit on the door
I'm sewn up neat in a canvas sheet
And I shan't be home no more.

H.M.S. *Glory*

CHARLES CAUSLEY

'Guz' is Naval slang for Devonport
'Aggie Weston's' is the familiar term used by sailors to describe the
hostels founded in many seaports by Dame Agnes Weston

Survivors

With the ship burning in their eyes
The white faces float like refuse
In the darkness—the water screwing
Oily circles where the hot steel lies.

They clutch with fingers frozen into claws
The lifebelts thrown from a destroyer,
And see, between the future's doors,
The gasping entrance of the sea.

Taken on board as many as lived, who
Had a mind left for living and the ocean,
They open eyes running with surf,
Heavy with the grey ghosts of explosion.

The meaning is not yet clear,
Where daybreak died in the smile—
And the mouth remained stiff
And grinning, stupid for a little while.

But soon they joke, easy and warm,
As men will who have died once
Yet somehow were able to find their way—
Muttering this was not included in their pay.

Later, sleepless at night, the brain spinning
With cracked images, they won't forget
The confusion and the oily dead,
Nor yet the casual knack of living.

                                             ALAN ROSS

Beach Burial

Softly and humbly to the Gulf of Arabs
The convoys of dead sailors come;
At night they sway and wander in the waters far under,
But morning rolls them in the foam.

Between the sob and clubbing of the gun fire
Someone, it seems, has time for this,
To pluck them from the shallows and bury them in
    burrows
And tread the sand upon their nakedness;

And each cross, the driven stake of tidewood,
Bears the last signature of men,
Written with such perplexity, with such bewildered pity,
The words choke as they begin—

'*Unknown seaman*'—the ghostly pencil
Wavers and fades, the purple drips,
The breath of the wet season has washed their inscriptions
As blue as drowned men's lips,

Dead seamen, gone in search of the same landfall,
Whether as enemies they fought,
Or fought with us, or neither: the sand joins them together,
Enlisted on the other front.

El Alamein

KENNETH SLESSOR

Mediterranean War

Some say it isn't deep
But it's deep enough for me,
Don't write no address on my grave
But the Mediterranean Sea.

I shan't drift in to shore:
For they'll pickle me a treat.
And I shall walk in a tidy rig
Past the ships of many a fleet.

Ships you never heard of,
Fleets that went down in thunder:
And them old shipmates from all the wars
Sharing the Mediterranean plunder.

JOHN PUDNEY

III—The Airmen

The Heart To Carry On

Every morning from this home
I go to the aerodrome.
And at evening I return
Save when work is to be done.
Then we share the separate night
Half a continent apart.

Many endure worse than we:
Division means long years and seas.
Home and lover are contained,
Even cursed within their breast.

Leaving you now, with this kiss
May your sleep tonight be blest,
Shielded from the heart's alarms
Until morning I return.
Pray tomorrow I may be
Close, my love, within these arms,
And not lie dead in Germany.

BERTRAM WARR (KILLED IN ACTION, 1943)

Air Gunner

The eye behind this gun made peace
With a boy's eye which doubted, trembled.
Guileless in the mocking light
Of frontiers where death assembled.

Peace was as single as the dawn,
Flew straightly as the birds migrating,
Timelessly in tune with time,
Purposeful, uncalculating.

So boyish doubt was put away:
The man's eye and the boy's were one.
Mockery and death retreat
Before the eye behind this gun.

JOHN PUDNEY

Combat Report

Just then I saw the bloody Hun.
You saw the Hun? You, light and easy,
Carving the soundless daylight. *I was breezy
When I saw that Hun.* O wonder,
Pattern of stress, of nerve poise, flyer,
Overtaking time. *He came out under
Nine-tenths cloud, but I was higher.*
Did Michelangelo aspire,
Painting the laughing cumulus, to ride
The majesty of air. *He was a trier,
I'll give him that, the Hun.* So you convert
Ultimate sky to air speed, drift and cover:

Sure with the tricky tools of God and lover.
I let him have a sharp four-second squirt!
Closing to fifty yards. He went on fire.
Your deadly petals painted, you exert
A simple stature. Man-high, without pride,
You pick your way through heaven and the dirt.
He burnt out in the air: that's how the poor sod died.

JOHN PUDNEY

Handz Vos Mine Name

Handz vos mine name hand ha Cherman vos hi
Ven out mit von Carl hi vent for a fly.
Ve ver men hof the kultur there vos no doubt—
Becoss both hof us flew in han Albatross Scout.

Ve looked for B.E.s for to straffe mit our guns—
But ven hi saw Carl hi knew he vos duns
For right on his tail there ver two little Sops
Shooting Hushabye Baby, Carl's in der copse.

ANON. (R.F.C.)

The Death Of The
Ball-Turret Gunner

From my mother's sleep I fell into the State,
And I hunched in its belly till my wet fur froze.
Six miles from earth, loosed from its dream of life,
I woke to black flack and the nightmare fighters.
When I died they washed me out of the turret with a hose.

RANDALL JARRELL

IV—And The Civilians

The Spanish Hands

The Spanish hands are young and pitiful.
Captured by disciplined and certain men,
On their own farms
Dejectedly they stand. Manhood
Has not mastered yet their boy's material,
And in their forms
The land's hard-broken awkwardness is shown.

They will be shot. The guns point whiteless eyes
That blacken memories. Each weather of the earth
That had its manual sign
And earth's exactions made futility.
Those simple groups unchanged, the walls and trees
Of their habitual scene
Shall grant no recognition to their death.

The spade thrown down, utensils of the field
Daily familiar with their hands, discarded place;
And taken, implements
Of other kinds and for another use.
They rose against the nameless will of death,
Moving as winters will across their land,
Themselves to be the devastated yield
And ruined increment:
Knowing that in time's round
There would return for them no further season,
Balanced on arms and boughs, their lives' and summer
   unison.

L. J. YATES

Song Of The Austrians In Dachau

NOTE. Over the entrance to Dachau Concentration Camp stood the words
ARBEIT MACHT FREI! [WORK MAKES FREE]

Pitiless the barbed wire dealing
Death that round our prison runs,
And a sky that knows no feeling
Sends us ice and burning suns;
Lost to us the world of laughter,
Lost our homes, our loves, our all:
Through the dawn our thousands muster,
To their work in silence fall.

> *But the slogan of Dachau is burnt on our brains*
> *And unyielding as steel we shall be;*
> *Are we men, brother? Then we'll be men when they've done.*
> *Work on, we'll go through the task we've begun,*
> *For work, brother, work makes us free.*

Haunted by the gun mouths turning
All our days and nights are spent;
Toil is ours—the way we're learning
Harder than we ever dreamt;
Weeks and months we cease to reckon
Pass, and some forget the years,
And so many men are broken
And their faces charged with fears.

> *But the slogan of Dachau is burnt on our brains*
> *And unyielding as steel we shall be;*
> *Are we men, brother? Then we'll be men when they've done.*
> *Work on, we'll go through with the task we've begun,*
> *For work, brother, work makes us free.*

Heave the stone and drag the truck,
Let no load's oppression show,
In your days of youth and luck
You thought lightly: now you know.
Plunge your spade in earth and shovel
Pity where heart cannot feel,
Purged in your own sweat and trouble
Be yourself like stone and steel.

But the slogan of Dachau is burnt on our brains
And unyielding as steel we shall be;
Are we men, brother? Then we'll be men when they've done.
Work on, we'll go through the task we've begun,
For work, brother, work makes us free.

One day sirens will be shrieking
One more roll-call, but the last.
And the stations we'll be seeking—
Outside, brother, prison past!
Bright the eyes of freedom burning,
Worlds to build with joy and zest
And the work begun that morning,
Yes, that work will be our best!

But the slogan of Dachau is burnt on our brains
And unyielding as steel we shall be;
Are we men, brother? Then we'll be men when they've done.
Work on, we'll go through with the task we've begun,
For work, brother, work makes us free.

GEORG ANDERS (Jura Soyfer)
(translated by John Lehmann)

Death Of An Aircraft

AN INCIDENT OF THE CRETAN CAMPAIGN, 1941
(TO GEORGE PSYCHOUNDAKIS)

One day on our village in the month of July
An aeroplane sank from the sea of the sky,
  White as a whale it smashed on the shore
  Bleeding oil and petrol all over the floor.

The Germans advanced in the vertical heat
To save the dead plane from the people of Crete,
  And round the glass wreck in a circus of snow
  Set seven mechanical sentries to go.

Seven stalking spiders about the sharp sun
Clicking like clockwork and each with a gun,
  But at *Come to the Cookhouse* they wheeled about
  And sat down to sausages and sauerkraut.

Down from the mountain burning so brown
Wriggled three heroes from Kastelo town,
  Deep in the sand they silently sank
  And each struck a match for a petrol-tank.

Up went the plane in a feather of fire
As the bubbling boys began to retire
  And, grey in the guardhouse, seven Berliners
  Lost their stripes as well as their dinners.

Down in the village, at murder-stations,
The Germans fell in friends and relations:
  But not a Kastelian snapped an eye
  As he spat in the air and prepared to die.

Not a Kastelian whispered a word
Dressed with the dust to be massacred,
   And squinted up at the sky with a frown
   As three bubbly boys came walking down.

One was sent to the county gaol
Too young for bullets if not for bail,
   But the other two were in prime condition
   To take on a load of ammunition.

In Archontiki they stood in the weather
Naked, hungry, chained together:
   Stark as the stones in the market-place,
   Under the eyes of the populace.

Their irons unlocked as their naked hearts
They faced the squad and their funeral-carts.
   The Captain cried, 'Before you're away
   Is there any last word you'd like to say?'

'I want no words,' said one, 'with my lead,
Only some water to cool my head.'
   'Water,' the other said, 'is all very fine
   But I'll be taking a glass of wine.

'A glass of wine for the afternoon
With permission to sing a signature-tune!'
   And he ran the *raki* down his throat
   And took a deep breath for the leading note.

But before the squad could shoot or say
Like the impala he leapt away
   Over the rifles, under the biers,
   The bullets rattling round his ears.

'Run!' they cried to the boy of stone
Who now stood there in the street alone,
   But, 'Rather than bring revenge on your head
   It is better for me to die,' he said.

The soldiers turned their machine-guns round
And shot him down with a dreadful sound
   Scrubbed his face with perpetual dark
   And rubbed it out like a pencil mark.

But his comrade slept in the olive tree
And sailed by night on the gnawing sea,
   The soldier's silver shilling earned
   And, armed like an archangel, returned.

CHARLES CAUSLEY

Swing-Song

I'm only a wartime working girl,
The machine shop makes me deaf,
I have no prospects after the war
And *my* young man is in the R.A.F.
   K for Kitty calling P for Pru . . .
   Bomb Doors Open . . .
   Over to You.

Night after night as he passes by
I wonder what he's gone to bomb
And I fancy in the jabber of the mad machines
That I hear him talking on the intercomm.
>   K for Kitty calling P for Prue . . .
>   Bomb Doors Open . . .
>   Over to You.

So there's no one in the world, I sometimes think,
Such a wall flower as I
For I must talk to myself on the ground
While he is talking to his friends in the sky:
>   K for Kitty calling P for Prue . . .
>   Bomb Doors Open . . .
>   Over to You.

LOUIS MACNEICE

The Hero

'Jack fell as he'd have wished,' the Mother said,
And folded up the letter that she'd read.
'The Colonel writes so nicely.' Something broke
In the tired voice that quavered to a choke.
She half looked up. 'We mothers are so proud
Of our dead soldiers.' Then her face was bowed.

Quietly the Brother Officer went out.
He'd told the poor old dear some gallant lies
That she would nourish all her days, no doubt.
For while he coughed and mumbled, her weak eyes
Had shone with gentle triumph, brimmed with joy,
Because he'd been so brave, her glorious boy.

He thought how 'Jack', cold-footed, useless swine,
Had panicked down the trench that night the mine
Went up at Wicked Corner; how he'd tried
To get sent home, and how, at last, he died,
Blown to small bits. And no one seemed to care
Except that lonely woman with white hair.

SIEGFRIED SASSOON

Bombing Casualties In Spain

Dolls' faces are rosier but these were children
their eyes not glass but gleaming gristle
dark lenses in whose quicksilver glances
the sunlight quivered. These blenched lips
were warm once and bright with blood
but blood
held in a moist bleb of flesh
not spilt and spatter'd in tousled hair.

In these shadowy tresses
red petals did not always
thus clot and blacken to a scar.

These are dead faces.
Wasps' nests are not so wanly waxen
wood embers not so greyly ashen.

They are laid out in ranks
like paper lanterns that have fallen
after a night of riot
extinct in the dry morning air.

HERBERT READ

The Assertion

Now, in the face of destruction,
In the face of the woman knifed out of all recognition
By flying glass, the fighter spinning like vertigo
On the axis of the trapped pilot and crowds applauding,
Famine that bores like a death-watch deep below,
Notice of agony splashed on headline and hoarding,
In the face of the infant burned
To death, and the shattered ship's-boat low in the trough—
Oars weakly waving like a beetle overturned—
Now, as never before, when man seems born to hurt
And a whole wincing earth not wide enough
For his ill will, now is the time we assert
To their face that men are love.

For love's no laughing matter,
Never was a free gift, an angel, a fixed equator.
Love's the big boss at whose side for ever slouches
The shadow of the gunman: he's mortar and dynamite;
Antelope, drinking pool, but the tiger too that crouches.
Therefore be wise in the dark hour to admit
The logic of the gunman's trigger,
Embrace the explosive element, learn the need
Of tiger for antelope and antelope for tiger.

O love, so honest of face, so unjust in action,
Never so dangerous as when denied,
Let your kindness tell us how false we are, your bloody
    correction
Our purpose and our pride.

                                        C. DAY LEWIS

The Streets Of Laredo

O early one morning I walked out like Agag,
Early one morning to walk through the fire
Dodging the pythons that leaked on the pavements
With twinkle of glasses and tangle of wire;

When grimed to the eyebrows I met an old fireman
Who looked at me wryly and thus did he say:
'The streets of Laredo are closed to all traffic,
We won't never master this joker today.

'O hold the branch tightly and wield the axe brightly,
The bank is in powder, the banker's in hell,
But loot is still free on the streets of Laredo
And when we drive home we drive home on the bell.'

Then out from a doorway there sidled a cockney,
A rocking-chair rocking on top of his head:
'O fifty-five years I been feathering my love-nest
And look at it now—why, you'd sooner be dead.'

At which there arose from a wound in the asphalt,
His big wig a-smoulder, Sir Christopher Wren
Saying: 'Let them make hay in the streets of Laredo;
When your ground-rents expire I will build them again.'

Then twangling their bibles with wrath in their nostrils
From Bunhill Fields came Bunyan and Blake:
'Laredo the golden is fallen, is fallen;
Your flame shall not quench nor your thirst shall not
    slake.'

'I come to Laredo to find me asylum',
Says Tom Dick and Harry the Wandering Jew;
'They tell me report at the first police station
But the station is pancaked—so what can I do?'

Thus eavesdropping sadly I strolled through Laredo
Perplexed by the dicta misfortunes inspire
Till one low last whisper inveigled my earhole—
The voice of the Angel, the voice of the fire:

O late, very late, have I come to Laredo
A whimsical bride in my new scarlet dress
But at last I took pity on those who were waiting
To see my regalia and feel my caress.

Now ring the bells gaily and play the hose daily,
Put splints on your legs, put a gag on your breath;
O you streets of Laredo, you streets of Laredo,
Lay down the red carpet—My dowry is death.

LOUIS MACNEICE

The Fury Of Aerial Bombardment

You would think the fury of aerial bombardment
Would rouse God to relent; the infinite spaces
Are still silent. He looks on shock-pride faces.
History, even, does not know what is meant.

You would feel that after so many centuries
God would give man to repent; yet he can kill
As Cain could, but with multitudinous will,
No farther advanced than in his ancient furies.

Was man made stupid to see his own stupidity?
Is God by definition indifferent, beyond us all?
Is the eternal truth man's fighting soul
Wherein the Beast ravens in its own avidity?

Of Van Wettering I speak, and Averill,
Names on a list, whose faces I do not recall
But they are gone to early death, who late in school
Distinguished the belt feed lever from the belt holding pawl.

RICHARD EBERHART

Thoughts During An Air Raid

Of course, the entire effort is to put oneself
Outside the ordinary range
Of what are called statistics. A hundred are killed
In the outer suburbs. Well, well, one carries on.
So long as this thing 'I' is propped up on
The girdered bed which seems so like a hearse,
In the hotel bedroom with the wall-paper
Blowing smoke-wreaths of roses, one can ignore
The pressure of those names under the fingers
Indented by lead type on newsprint,
In the bar, the marginal wailing wireless.
Yet supposing that a bomb should dive
Its nose right through this bed, with one upon it?
The thought's obscene. Still, there are many
For whom one's loss would illustrate
The 'impersonal' use indeed. The essential is
That every 'one' should remain separate

Propped up under roses, and no one suffer
For his neighbour. Then horror is postponed
Piecemeal for each, until it settles on him
That wreath of incommunicable grief
Which is all mystery or nothing.

STEPHEN SPENDER

Man, Take Your Gun

Man, take your gun: and put to shame
earthquake and plague, the acts of God.
You maim the crazy and the lame.

Terror is their palsy, the knees
of men buckle for fear of man.
You are the God whom frenzy pleases.

You are the gas-man, and the flier
who drops his bomb; the man in tanks.
You wire mines and fear the fire.

And dig the hollow street with trenches
the gas-mains and the sewer cross.
The stench of dead men makes you flinch.

But if the dying whimper, pain
pricks you like courage, like delight.
The veins sing to the cruel brain.

What are you, man, that gun in hand
with savagery and pity go,
and face to face with madness stand;

and acid-drenched and poison-sprayed
see flame run lovely like a wake
from raiders; and the burning lake
shake overhead? You are afraid.

The shadow flickers on the wall
like morse, like gun-shot. Terror walks
the tall roofs where the snipers hawk.
He stalks you, man. And, man, you fall.

J. BRONOWSKI